PRAISE FOR EARLIER BOOKS

"A well-pruned, wonderfully illustrated abridgment. A gripping retelling of the classic."—The 'Wishing Shelf' Book Review of *The Legend of Sleepy Hollow*

"Pathan's incredibly varied collection of 21 stories covers the gamut of LGBTQ issues and the hurdles individuals face. . . . This volume's exhaustive approach to elevating queer issues remains commendable."—Kirkus Review of *The Love That Dare Not Speak Its Name: Short Stories*

"Fast-paced and intense, this book is well plotted and will keep readers turning pages."—The Booklife Prize Review of *Amina: The Silent One*

"A heartfelt story of great resilience in the face of overwhelming odds *NIRMALA: The Mud Blossom* is Fiza Pathan at her very best."—Book Viral Review of *NIRMALA: The Mud Blossom*

"A bible for anybody working with children's literature. Fascinating and informative." —A 'Wishing Shelf' Book Review of *CLASSICS: Why and how we can encourage children to read them*

"A clever retelling of Carroll's classic story with all the imagery of the original."—A 'Wishing Shelf' Book Review of *Through the Looking-Glass: And What Alice Found There*

The Reclusive Writer
& Reader of Bandra

The Reclusive Writer & Reader of Bandra

essays

Fiza Pathan

Fiza Pathan Publishing OPC Private Limited

Mumbai, INDIA

Imprint. Freedom With Pluralism®
Fiza Pathan Publishing OPC Private Limited
2 Symbol Apts., Tertullian Rd, Off Dr. Peter Dias Road.
Bandra West, Mumbai 400050, INDIA
Email. fizapathan@fizapathanpublishing.com

Editor. Kimberly Catanzarite.
Author's caricature drawn by illustrator Farzana Cooper.
Image is copyrighted. © 2018
Cover art and design: LLPix Photography & Design.

Author's Note: This is a work of nonfiction. I have tried to recreate events, locales, and conversation from my memories of them. I recognize that the memories of people described in this book may be different from my own. It is also possible that my recollection and interpretation of events may not be entirely objective. In order to maintain their anonymity in some instances I have omitted mention of names of individuals as my intention was not to hurt them. This book should be treated as a combination of facts about my life and certain embellishments. It is not my intention to malign any person or institution. The reader should not consider this book anything other than a work of literature.

Publisher's Disclaimer: The above work is published as submitted by the author on an as-is basis without assuming any liability whatsoever: legal, financial or otherwise. Both the publisher and author regret any unintentional harm resulting from the publishing and marketing of *The Reclusive Writer & Reader of Bandra: Essays*.

Book Layout © 2017 BookDesignTemplates.com

Book Title/Author. The Reclusive Writer & Reader of Bandra: Essays. Pathan, Fiza -- 1st ed

ISBN 978-8-1938201-3-1 Hardcover
ISBN 978-8-1938201-2-4 Paperback
ISBN 978-8-1938201-4-8 E-book

For Nana

Nowadays, I know the true reason I read is to feel less alone, to make a connection with a consciousness other than my own.

–ZADIE SMITH

contents

introductory essay

My father didn't want me because I was a girl.

I was born on the nineteenth of March 1989 to my parents in Bandra West, Mumbai, India. After a few months of shuffling from my mother's place to my father's and vice versa, my maternal grandmother, who spoke very little English as she was only in school till the third grade, told my father that my mother wasn't a puppet on the string and that I would be brought up forever at my mother's place. I live here to this day, though my grandmother has long gone to her eternal rest.

So Grandmother settled it, and me too, in her home in Bandra West, the queen of the Mumbai suburbs. I was baptized a Catholic when I was two years old in the Basilica of Mount Mary's itself.

Needless to say, though I have to, my father did not observe my baptism. He was a hard-core Sunni Muslim, and very much in love with my mother.

It was me he did not much care for. I was a girl. Not a boy. And that was all.

The day I learned this fact was the day I withdrew into myself.

What do you, dear reader, surmise? That I would become some sort of an activist or a hard-core badass feminist? I'm not the type. I withdrew into myself, into my books, and into the places in Mumbai that have given me shelter and have acted as a wall between the swirling crowd of the city that never sleeps.

These places have mostly been libraries, bookshops, and writing huts. I have lived in solitude in these places, but I've never been alone.

Mumbai is the commercial capital of India. Mumbai, where you find the bones and flesh of aborted fetus in dustbins and food (which if you could remove properly could make a decent meal) thrown in there at the same time. Mumbai, where dreams come true. Mumbai, whose concrete roads reek with the smell of those who died in encounters with the police force or the Mafia. Mumbai, where every night is a party and where tourists from all over the world flock to see its historic structures. Mumbai, the city that you think you know, but which I have never known.

My Mumbai is different. My Mumbai is unique.

My Mumbai resides in places of solitude, where librarians stir their cups of tea with their index finger while I gaze at the new books and some old favorites lined up on the shelf.

My world is simple, economic, and very much devoted to contemplation.

I teach, write, and publish my stories, but still remain distant and anonymous. Isn't that a part of what a city does to you? It gives you a chance to do whatever you like and to remain anonymous while doing so. Mumbai has done that for me, and I am highly in its debt.

Thank you, Mumbai, for accepting me when my father threw his hands up at my mother thus ridding her finally of an obsessive husband and me of a gender-biased father. Thank you for giving me shelter, Grandmother, or "Nana," as I used to call her, and calling out to me even though you forgot what I looked like as you had lost your memory.

Thank you, Nana. Wish I had known you better. Thank you for giving me a place in your home in Bandra West, the Catholic region which comprises of British heritage cottages, numerous churches, pork markets, and many circulating libraries.

Thank you, Mother, or as I still call you, Mama, for educating me and teaching me my first alphabets. Thank you for making me go to school, college, and teacher's college where I rummaged through many books on the shelves of their libraries. I was trying to search for a story that was like my own. I found not only one or two but many, and they have been great comforts to me. Thank you, Mama.

Thank you, Mumbai, for having so many places where a bookworm like me can sit, have a cup of coffee, and write a short story on a writing pad or read yet another book of essays by Ruskin Bond, the Anglo-Indian writer from India's hills. Thank you for these modest places that have shaped me, a fatherless girl, into something decent, though I wish I could do better if only for your sake.

Lastly, thank you, Father, or as I used to call you, Papa, for the pain you've bequeathed to Mama and me. Mama is much better off without you, but I know she still loves you. As for me, if it were not for you, never would I have been to the places I have been and done the things I have done, which have shaped me into the writer, teacher, and reader I am. I cannot lie and say that I did not hate you for doing what you did. But if it were not for you, then these words wouldn't have ever been written in the first place. Here is a poem for you, Papa:

The wound you have darned in stitches on my brow,
That cut has made me beautiful, if not in face then at least in words;
I will keep this stigma ever in your memory,
Always be the daughter you left behind like a crown on my head.

Thank you places and books.

These essays are all for you that made me somewhat like you when I lived in you.

You.

Me.

Places.

2

queen of the suburbs

"You live in Bandra na? So lucky yaar! Do you see the Bollywood stars everyday? Tell na yaar!"

I have mentioned earlier that Bandra West is considered to be the Queen of the Mumbai suburbs. I've also mentioned that if now, in Bandra, you picked a rock and just throw it randomly it would definitely fall on a church. But it will also one hundred percent fall on a Bollywood celebrity, business magnate, or someone wanting to see the aforementioned people. ... Give me a break!

Bandra West was once a home to pigs, cows, buffalos, bungalows, cottages, churches, Christian schools, and the famous Bandra Bazaar, where most of the shoppers go if they want to buy just about anything. We've even got a heck of a lot of roads like Hill Road, Linking Road, Turner Road, et al. dedicated to shoppers and tourists where yet again something, anything and everything is sold.

It seems everyone in Mumbai DREAMS of being a resident of Bandra West in their next birth. Because if the prices are what they are now, no common man other than a multi-billionaire can afford even a 1 BHK (Bedroom Hall Kitchen) here for a decent price. A decent 1 BHK in Bandra West starts at ₹2.2 crores or approximately 300,000 dollars. ... Let's just forget about everything else.

Then comes the people who were already here before the place became too expensive to live in, or the people who came here in the early seventies when you could at least afford a pokey 1 BHK, example my house for ₹70,000 or approximately 8,000 dollars calculated at the rate of exchange existing in 1977!

My maternal family falls in the second category. They were from Byculla, a predominant Christian and Muslim locality in the town area of Mumbai, then Bombay City. They came to Bandra West with the help of a small loan from one of the famous yesteryear's Bollywood actor's sister. My mother repaid in installments the ₹20,000 loan after we shifted in; the major portion was paid slab wise in monthly/quarterly installments. And this is the place we now call home, the only roof over our heads.

Let me mention here that the same house if we think of selling it is worth ₹3 crores and even more because of its prime location near Mt. Mary's Basilica!

We, however, are always living in fear of somebody coming, the dubious builders or the autocratic government, to throw us out of our own home so that they may redevelop the place or create a road linking it to the main road towards Mt. Mary's, which is a prime pilgrimage site of the Christians in Mumbai, or builders who could swindle us out of our money by crooked means with the assistance of antisocial elements or the law, even though we pay our dues and our taxes good and proper as they say, and throw us out on the streets.

I only want a decent place to read, teach, and write in peace.

I'm only glad that we are not too near Bandstand, which is right near the sea, where the Richie Richest of the Rich stay, because, I've been reading the book of Revelations, the prophecies of Nostradamus and the lot, and I DON'T WANT

MY PRECIOUS BOOKS TO BE SUBMERGED UNDER WATER!

It's needless to say that, of course, I hate water, but I am still saying it for reasons of clarification.

Yes- yes -yes, I know that Bandra West is the suburb of the fisher folk, beaches, and beautiful seaside sunrises and sunsets, but already I've told you my feelings about anything that is liquid—I fear for my books.

So, if you are thinking that I am going to write a piece about the wonderful effect the Arabian Sea has had on me for twenty-nine years, you can just forget it. I hate the sea. I hate water. Nasty stuff, this sea thing. ... Why ever did God or the Devil make it in the first place!?

And no, I don't like watching movies, television, iPad, iPod, whatever at all either so that implies that I don't care a hang about the Bollywood 'booty-fool' people who live here. Most of the time I don't even recognize them until someone with bated breath and selfie camera aglow points them out to me.

I know a few because of a certain sadistic pleasure I used to get of seeing certain sadistic movies of Bollywood in the 1990s, which were copied from certain sadistic movies of Hollywood of the entire twentieth century. You know, the homicidal maniac who kills only girls; the obsessive boy lover writing the name of his lady love with a knife on his naked chest; fiancés dropping off their to-be wives from the top of high-rise buildings; men being stabbed with knife, dagger, broken bottle shards, spears, iron poles, and pointed rods and yet not dying until they bleed their last words on the laps of their woeful widow mothers, with lots of blood like paan juice being emitted from their wounds but ... you get my drift.

No, give me a Ruskin Bond book any day.

I rarely go out, unless it's for research or it's to a bookshop/library. I'm sure I would be very happy to be locked up in a single room for the rest of my life as long I was given a Kindle Fire with unlimited battery power and billions of rupees to spend on buying Kindle books. I would spend my entire life just sitting there in that room, reading. Just give me food, water, and a clean English toilet with running water on a regular basis, if you want me to survive.

Otherwise, what is more glorious than to die next to a pile of books you were wanting to read?

So, if you think that I'm going to tell you about how I have personality traits or identities from places, as in, places other than books then you better forget about it, for I do nothing other than read, teach, and write (in order in matter of importance to my existence).

But, yes, certain places have led me to more books and have had a subtle effect on my personality, which I will dwell upon in this book of essays.

I'm not saying I am a prude and absolutely incorrigible, but if you get that idea then you're near my line of thought.

If you think that you would not know what you know if it were not for the books you have read, then you can peruse these little essays about the only places I only really go to without being under compulsion: bookshops and libraries.

I have loathed to travel ever since I was a toddler. I used to vomit in taxies and accidently fall out of moving rickshaws.

I have this demonic *urge of old* to visit the toilet every few hours, which makes long-distance traveling a pain in the groin.

I once kept my urine and crap on hold all the way from Bangalore to Mysore. That was the first and last time I traveled by road. I was trying to locate R. K. Narayan's home in Mysore, my all-time favorite writer, who was the creator of the South Indian fictional town of Malgudi. I found his house but couldn't stay there long enough because I had to pee badly.

Sorry, master, Grand old man of Malgudi!

But I kept a plastic bag full of the sand from his broken-down bookshelf. It has brought me luck and is still with me. I plan on keeping it for the rest of my bookish life, unless we have to *run for it* if a tsunami hits our turf. That's why I prefer landlocked regions which are not near the vicinity of water or a volcano or on an earthquake belt … and there are plenty of such wondrous places in India. Some of them are our cool and humble hill stations.

I've never been to any of India's hill stations before, and yet because of my second favorite writer's works, Ruskin Bond, I feel that in a way, I too belong to the mountains, and the land of the simple hill station is my true home.

That's just one of the ways books make you feel a part of a place you have never been to in all your life, but you know that there it is, your real home. It is one of my greater wishes to spend the last days of my life, if I live that long, at a hill station, most preferably at the places where my writer mentor used to live, Dehradun, Mussoorie, Shimla, etc.

So these little essays are not about places of grandeur or of historical importance. These are the essays that are the truth of my simple, mundane, and yet, fulfilling life, for now at least.... The storm is arriving.

My country is in unrest. As I pen these essays, a FOURTEEN-MONTH-OLD infant was recently raped, and because of certain bizarre circumstances and the way things are culminating in the Post-truth era, there are riots in Gujarat, the neighbor of Maharashtra—my state.

Lynching, murder, religious intolerance, caste riots, regionalism, suppression of the press, and all the worst possible calumny against man is a part of our lives here in India these past five years as we move on to the next Lok Sabha elections in 2019. I don't know about you, but thank heavens I'm stocked with enough books to last till all this mayhem blows over.

The places that I write about in these essays have taught me tolerance, unity in diversity, and shared existence, but I don't know whether these little libraries and bookshops of my past, which have shaped the person I am today, will outlast this wave of despotism and fascism.

step into the church

My story, not so long ago, begins with my maternal uncle, who I call by his first name, Blaise, without the formality of the prefix or suffix *uncle*, who is a bachelor and who used to bring me comics from a lending library called "Step-In," down the road from our home and next to our parish church, St. Francis of Assisi.

I was already growing into a reclusive and solitary soul. I played alone, mostly on my cycle. If I ever played with the neighborhood children, it was only because I wanted to tell stories at the end of a hide-and-seek game or a catching cook session.

Everyone loved to hear the stories I used to tell, especially my horror stories. I was good at giving people a fright.

I used to play on my red potty, with toys all around me, when Blaise would come home from his work at the bank or from the church, with a comic in his backpack. I did so love those comics, and they gave me ideas for stories that I used to pretend I could write on my Macintosh, because I wasn't even three years old, you see, and I hadn't learned anything about writing properly yet.

But I could read. Well, sort of. I used to gaze at the comic book characters and gauge by their expressions what situation they were probably in. I loved to make up situations. It used to give me a kick.

I loved reading while sitting on my potty. The comic books from Step-In were my staple diet. I went to church every day and came back in time to say the rosary with Nana and the rest, and then I went to my books.

Anyone growing up in 1990s Bandra West can remember the large quantity of their time spent at their respective parish churches. There was a saying that if you randomly threw a rock in any direction in Bandra, it would either fall on a pig or a church; there were that many churches in the suburbs.

Naturally I was a good Catholic toddler, going to church every day, and my favorite church was our own parish church, St. Francis of Assisi.

The church was like something from a fairy tale, one of those places I used to read about in books borrowed from the Step-In library. The church was near the Bandra seaside cemetery and near the Jewish cemetery, which gave it a really sinister appearance at night. The church itself was hidden in a huge foliage of grass and woodland with cows, pigs, and goats tethered all over the place by the neighboring Gujarati Catholics, who were the main parishioners of the church.

"Why is that man helping Jesus down?" I once asked seeing the statue of St. Francis of Assisi holding the stigmatized body of Jesus.

"He was a good man," was the reply Mama gave me and went back to saying her rosary before the mass could start. I knelt down on the marble floor and prostrated myself before the statue the way a Muslim prays.

To my surprise, I got a whack for doing so.

The entire of my preschool life was spent at that church or reading comics or fairy tales from the Step-In lending library.

I loved all the popular comics: *Asterix, Tintin, Phantom, Archie, Mandrake: The Magician,*

Spiderman, and *Batman*. When Batman meets St. Francis of Assisi in the mind of a toddler who doesn't have a father, the effect is naturally bizarre—and so it was for me. I was very much a fervent Christian and loved it when the bad guys got their just desserts in the end.

That's what I like about the comics and those are the stories I used to tell my toddler friends. They liked those stories too, and we used to play act them in the compound of our 1970s building or on the staircase, pretending we were poor as church mice and that we hardly had enough money to place food on the table, but that after we died, we would become saints through the power of Jesus Christ.

I used to say the rosary every day. Everybody in Bandra used to say the rosary every day. It was part and parcel of being a resident of Bandra.

But there was another side of this humble Christian society that would stifle my voice into silence. You see, single mothers are looked down upon in Christian society, and so was my mama. I was a fatherless girl, and this community of Catholics never let me forget it.

"Hello, baby, where is your papa? Why he not come to see you?"

"Hello, baby, tell mama to make you Catholic so you don't stay Muslim like Papa."

"Hello, baby, Fiza, why you go to church? Go back to Papa and take Mama there na; that's where you should be. Fiza, Mama, and Papa – Jesus, Mary, and Joseph na?"

Catholic women, while either coming back from church or going to church, used to peep in at our door and abuse my mama, telling her that it was a sin to live without her husband and that I had to be baptized or she would be further punished. Mama used to close the door and swallow her rage. I too seethed with anger, but at that age I never really understood what the matter was.

All I knew was that everyone in Bandra went to church and that one day soon I would go to school. School would be in Mahim, very far away, where my building friends never went. They all said it was not a good place to study, because it was Protestant.

"They don't pray to Mother Mary there you know," chirped one of my older playmates who knew how to ride on a cycle without the side wheels and who was not using the potty any more.

"Don't go there," she said. "Come to my school. It's a good Catholic school. We can play there during the breaks."

I nodded to her and by the time I was four years and three months old, I was admitted to Bombay Scottish School, Mahim. Mama wouldn't hear my protest. She worked there as a teacher and junior supervisor, and it would be a privilege for me to study in such a rich school practically for free. So what if it was a Protestant school? It would make a good girl out of me.

My playmate was dejected that I didn't join the local Catholic school and had to travel in rich cars of other rich children as a part of the car pool to get to school. But I couldn't rid myself of the Catholic Bandra effect. Whenever I would come back from school, I would make the sign of the cross at every passing stone cross and church of which there were plenty.

Name of the Father, Son, and Holy Spirit – Name of The Father, Son and Holy Spirit – Name of the Father, Son and Holy Spirit!

"Why you not go to good decent Catholic school, baby? Why you go to there where your friend not go?"

"Where is Papa? Fiza baby is dirty girl. She has no Papa."

"Where is your papa Fiza doll? Why he no come to take you with him to his home?"

I was disturbed by these questions, for which I didn't have any good answers. No matter how hard I tried to be a Catholic in Bandra, it did not work, especially not when I was a toddler. But Bandra made me a Catholic. It did what very few used to do back in the 1990s: it made a Muslim father's child into a Catholic Christian, and I was always gazed upon with eyes of wonder and at the same time with eyes of contempt.

Today I am twenty-nine years old, a teacher, writer, and publisher. I'm unmarried and still a virgin. Bandra has changed a lot with the age of artificial intelligence and insecurity among minorities. Crosses have been broken down by the BMC and threats are being made to Catholic, Muslim, and Parsee graveyards to be razed to let in more space for the teeming traffic and the teeming hordes of people coming to Bandra to see and witness this beautiful green suburb where Catholics live as a large majority still and where though now if you throw a rock it won't hit a pig but it will surely still hit a church. The churches and some of the chapels and crosses of the earlier centuries are still here.

I am an existentialist these days, but I still like and practice the Catholic way of life. In my office-cum-writing hut there is a three-foot statue of St. Francis of Assisi, whom I kiss on the lips before I start my typing or writing for the day.

Mama is retired and so is Blaise. But Step-In is still there and the owner Prakash uncle still remembers those days when Blaise used to carry in his backpack piles of comics for me to read. My library number is still etched in my memory; it's 422, and it's more holy to me these days than the Trinity.

Mama goes to church every day, and I wish I could but I am too busy with work. We Catholics strangely are a quiet lot here in Bandra West, and I think I have somewhat imbibed that quality of our church, St. Francis of Assisi, into my system.

Silence, contemplation, and fervent prayers—these make Bandra West a place of pilgrimage, especially during the month of September when we celebrate the birthday of Mother Mary and during other Marian feast days, which are celebrated with a lot of pomp and splendor.

I keep away from it all and stay locked up in my writing hut, penning stories, essays, and character sketches. I sometimes visit lending libraries and bookshops in town. Nowhere else.

I live in a land of a pious community, and as long as I have a good book or pen with paper beside me, I am content to live out at least my youth in Bandra. Afterward, I wish to spend retirement in the hills of India, like my second favorite writer, Ruskin Bond, the famous writer from the hills. Though I live very much in the flat lands, in the plains of Maharashtra, the land of the warrior Marathas, it is Ruskin Bond's writings that has made me yearn for the hills.

4

step-in circulating library

tep-In is a lending library on St. John the Baptist Road in Bandra West near the parish of St. Francis of Assisi. It's run by a Sindhi gentleman who is also a real estate agent. His name is Prakash, and he is older than Blaise, who is sixty-one. I've known him even before I went to school.

I read mostly comics from his library and then graduated to reading R. L. Stine horror books, especially books in the Goosebumps and Fear Street series. Then onto Roald Dahl books, the classics and then some anthologies of ghost and vampire stories.

Step-In was right at the junction of two streets and so had many customers, when I was a kid, especially for his comics. Blaise swears even to this day that even before I could read, I understood the comics I used to flip through. He even said that I used to pretend to write stories when I did not even know how to write. I used to "write" these squiggles that resembled an adult's mature writing style on my mackintoshes, on the walls of our home, and in writing pads no longer in use.

Every day I went to church and on my way back, I stopped at Step-In, or Blaise, on my behalf, would go there to pick a comic or an abridged classic for me, which the owner had in plenty. I used to spend my days reading through the books of the lending library instead of playing with the other children who lived in the building.

In fact, in my head I had created a world of my own based on people living in the locality of Bandra Mt. Mary's Basilica. It was a world in which I lived in a neighborhood and belonged to a motorcycle gang called "The Eagles," and we were always gathering clues, solving mysteries, and saving the neighborhood from the evil gang on the other side of town called "The West Side Scorpions."

I had actually played with these characters in my head rather than the real people in front of me. My teachers at school and my family realized that I was different, maybe even psychologically disturbed or mentally overactive.

All these ideas, as you may have guessed, were an admixture of the fiction from the Step-In library. I didn't know back then that it was the writer in me trying to come out into the open.

I would cycle for hours together during the Diwali vacations around my building compound imagining what sort of adventures 'The Eagles 'and I would have. In my bicycle basket would be copies of the latest R. L. Stine 'Fear Street' novel I planned to dig into as for hours together I used to circle the complex dressed in a thin summer dress. When Blaise used to come back from church, I would come back to the real world of Bandra West and go inside for dinner.

I had no friends. Well, no real friends. I had a whole neighborhood of make-believe people who were more meaningful to me than the kids at Bombay Scottish School or the neighborhood Christian kids.

Everyone was certain I was crazy. Some people even thought I was a victim of black magic perpetrated by my paternal grandmother, a woman whose face I cannot recall even today, and who, people believed, practiced the Black Arts. They said she wanted me to leave the church and become a Muslim.

That train of thought did not scare me. It was simply fuel I added to the white-hot fire of my imagination.

By the time I was in college, I stopped visiting Step-In and Prakash uncle. It was just as well, because after the floods in Mumbai in 2005, he had lost most of his stock, and when I passed John the Baptist Road the other day, he was making more money selling greeting cards and stationery.

Today Bandra looks really different from the pork farm that it was back when I was growing up and when my nana moved here with her brood—sans her husband who had died of diabetes and was interred in a graveyard in Byculla, which was my father's neighborhood, now an impoverished and backward Muslim neighborhood.

Christian—Muslim—Christian—Muslim—Christian—Muslim — that's all I've been hearing since I've ever known the difference between the two damn words.

I remember one birthday of mine, in 2001, when I was getting dressed to go to St. Francis of Assisi Church near the old stable or *tabela* of Bandra West, when my father arrived.

He was certainly not expected, and Mama and he created a ruckus. I had to lock myself in the common bedroom as my wild father threw himself at all the doors and windows of our home to get in and wish his only daughter *a very happy birthday*. He screamed and hollered. I was terrified. Mama managed to keep him out even though she was frail.

He left after banging at the common bedroom window. I was partially absent from the scene. I was mentally busy having an adventure with the Eagle gang while physically, I was crouched in a corner of the room, my hands over my head, trembling at the suddenness of the shock.

It took a whole mental adventure to calm me down. My mama promised me that he wouldn't come back and that he wouldn't take me away to Muslim Byculla to his witch of a mother. She said that I could go to Step-In with Blaise and buy a whole lot of Phantom and Mandrake the Magician comics after church like a good mama's Catholic girl.

But I did not go to St. Francis of Assisi that birthday. I went to another church down the road near the famous Lilavati Hospital, a church called "Mt. Carmel's Church," *just in case my father would be waiting in the cemetery at Assisi!*

Today, I no longer visit Prakash uncle. But I still visit the world his books created for me, and I ride with the Eagles.

bombay scottish school library

hated my school. I hated everyone related to it. I had no friends, and I was not wanted there.

But the school library, now that's a different story to tell.

The area that is a bridge between town Bombay and the suburbs with its salt pans is the Hindu-Muslim locality called Mahim. It was there, right near the Mahim Bay, that the Scottish missionaries of old built the school that was first an orphanage for the children of soldiers and other official staff of the British East India Company and later the British government in India.

It is a large heritage structure that is hailed even today as one of the best ICSE schools in

Mumbai and one of the most prestigious. It looks like a stone university, with a large garden, fields for sport, and a sizable playground for the middle school children.

I spent twelve miserable years there in that very same institution. It was co-ed, and I didn't get along with either sex.

But then I discovered the library.

It was natural that a bookworm like me should do so, but I was aided by the fact that we, at Scottish, had a separate library period every week where we went to the school library, which was large in size, vast in collection, and had high ceilings stacked with wooden bookshelves, something like Disney's *Beauty and the Beast* library.

For twelve years of my school life, I spent more than half of my time in that school library.

My only two friends were Mrs. Ratnaswami, the head librarian, and Aruna her one and only support staff, or matron of the library.

Mrs. Ratnaswami was the woman I admired and loved. It was she who first told me of the benefits of reading, encouraged me to make charts for the library, and most importantly, how to use my mama's library credit to fill my bookish needs.

"Pizza (she could never pronounce my name)," Mrs. Ratnaswami would exhale in her nasal voice full of patience. "Pizza—use mummy's card and then you can take any number of books that you like for any amount of time, okay?"

I used the card liberally. I was always roaming around in the library, reading the tomes bigger than my hands could contain.

The library was my fortress of old British stone. Just like the school was a bastion against the French in the nineteenth century and against the revolting Indians during the Mutiny of 1857, the stone edifice was like the father I did not have. It protected me from other students, teachers, and the drudgery of school life in 1990-2000s Mumbai.

The books on the shelves which I used to climb with the help of Mrs. Ratnaswami and Aruna were the nuggets of wisdom which a father should have shared with his daughter. That library was my protector, my support and ... yes ... my father.

And now it's more than just gone. But I'll speak of that a little later.

"This child is only reading books the whole day," complained Mrs. Ratnaswami to no one in particular on a regular basis as I read a classic like

Kim or *Treasure Island* or *Dracula*, my ultimate favorite. Aruna would dust the shelves and rearrange the books in correct order while I read in my corner of the expansive library, which at one point of time in history was the boarding room of the orphan European boys.

Mrs. Ratnaswami loved to have her tea. She took it with milk and three tablespoons of white sugar, which she stirred using her right index finger, though the liquid was piping hot. That index finger was rough as the hide of a rhinoceros.

Aruna never took tea, as she was like a library Cinderella, dusting a shelf here, mending a book spine there, keeping the mites out of the wood. She was always busy, and she liked it that way; after all, she was the only support staff who could read and write and understand and speak English, Marathi, and Hindi.

If she happened to be free, she would be seated in front of her favorite section in the library, the Hindi and Marathi section where she would be reading, totally engrossed, a story by Premchand or Saratchandra or Yashpal, or a biography in Marathi either of Nehru, Gandhi, Mother Teresa, or Rani Laxmibai.

These two women were the models of my childhood. While I observed them, I think I drowned myself in my prestigious school's library dust.

I was somber like the silent walls and full of bookish curiosity like the movable panels of the secret sections in the library. And there were many of those.

I discovered Charles Dickens in that library, along with a host of others books that I was actually not old enough to read but which I did all the same: William Makepeace Thackeray, Emily Dickinson, Robin Cook, P. G. Wodehouse, Rudyard Kipling, Ruskin Bond, Arthur Hailey, Thomas Hardy, Henry James, William Shakespeare, Munshi Premchand, Jane Austen, Bram Stoker, Sidney Sheldon, Graham Greene, Jules Verne, Guy De Maupassant, Saki, O. Henry, Katherine Mansfield, Dean Koontz, Edgar Allan Poe, V. S. Naipaul, Rabindranath Tagore, and so many others.

The school library was my second home, and I became a very eccentric individual because of the stuff I was reading every day and especially during the summer, Diwali, and Christmas vacations.

Our school rested on the former Cadel Road, which is now named after the revolutionary freedom fighter Veer Savarkar. It overlooked the Arabian Sea, which when viewed from any of the turrets of the school, could take your breath away.

Mumbai is indeed a coastal metropolis and the epicenter of Bollywood and fashion. But somehow I never took to it or got carried away by the Hollywood of Indian cinema. I was content to be a bookworm and searching the shelves of my school library for my next read.

The library was closed during the vacations; otherwise, I'm quite sure I wouldn't have ever stayed at home.

"Pizza, you are reading such small text. ... You'll soon need horn-rimmed spectacles for your eyes," said Mrs. Ratnaswami every time I checked out a Dickens paperback at the library counter. I loved filling out my mother's name on the library card, *Mrs. Pathan,* along with the date. Now I experience that same pleasure when I use the book app Goodreads and when I stamp with purple ink the date the book is issued or due at the libraries I visit.

Everyone at school kept their distance from me because of my unwillingness to talk to them or to start a conversation. I also was singled out for personal vengeance on the part of both teachers and students because my mama was a school coordinator. *... Can't take it out on the mother, then the daughter will do ...* that sort of thing.

My imagination knew no bounds at Scottish and it seemed that the studiousness of Mahim was having an affect me. I was always immersed in a study of something or the other and after I passed out of the school, I still made weekly trips from college in Bandra to Mahim to the library as long as my mama was teaching there.

Then in 2009, she retired, and a new principal was appointed. She debarred me from visiting the school library. I was depressed and inconsolable; that library was my second home ... my father.

It was in 2015 when I returned to the school to substitute for a teacher that I entered the library after a long and painful separation of six years.

Oodles of things can happen in that time. One of them was that the old tomes were no longer there. The floor-to-ceiling wooden bookshelves were gone as well. In their place were glass and steel office bookcases that made a hell of a noise when opened.

Mrs. Ratnaswami had retired and a new, very confused, coffee-loving librarian sat in her place. When Aruna heard I had come, she came to give me a tight hug. But we both knew what was missing between us. My father, the books, were gone ... eighteenth-century leather calf-bound volumes, nineteenth-century hardbacks, and rare first editions of authors and poets the world had long forgotten ... gone.

I had lost my father.

You didn't send me even a letter,
Now where have you gone beloved?
Where shall I search for you?
In these wooden panels are my first stirring letters.

I am supposed to write about the places that shaped my personality. How can you, dear reader, EVER FATHOM THE WORLDS THAT SLIPPED AWAY FROM ME SO CRUELY THAT DAY???!!!

Aruna lowered her head and went back to her dusting. I backed into my old corner and slumped into one of the new plastic chairs. I cried for the books gone far away and the places we'd conjured together in this dusty alcove of BSS. And I cried for those I had yet to read, the many places within their pages that I had not visited.

Am I to write about the places that have had a deep bearing on my personality? Then what about the places I've been and the wondrous things I have seen thanks to the magic combination of a writer's or poet's twenty-six alphabet letters? The places I've *seen* through the *eyes* of printer's black ink? Victorian London, World War One, the Holocaust, the Napoleonic Wars, Greece, the later Vedic period in India, Revolutionary France, the bubonic plague, Nero's Rome, Jesus' Jerusalem..., oh the places that I have been and the things I can relate which have touched my soul, while all the while to an onlooker I sat solemnly with a decanter of water nearby, on my wooden chair in my school library.

I've learned many things that have since become internalized in me. I've learned about extravagance from Lord Byron, about obsession from Mary Shelley, rage from St. Augustine, patience from Gandhi, the art of love from Jane Austen, grief from Edgar Allan Poe, statesmanship from Nehru, and so much more. And yet, do I really represent all these things? Do I?

What do I stand for after studying in Mumbai's topmost educational institution, the pride of ICSE? Nothing but a love to earn money by writing and teaching so that I can buy books and sit in one comfortable place for hours, reading. I don't display statesmanship by sipping lemon iced tea as I read through Tolstoy's *War and Peace*, nor do

I adhere to any ounce of chivalry as I turn a page of the tale of *Dracula*, nor perform innovative thinking as I adjust the recliner to read about Edward Rutherfurd's idea of the various cities I love, nor partake in love as unflinching I read page after page of the Holy Bible. ... No. ... All I really want is to spend my days interfering with no one in particular, teaching students who don't question my utterances, and hoping that at the end of a busy schedule I can at least get in three hours of reading before I go to bed.

These are the things that make me feel part of a place ninety-nine percent of the time, though I've never been physically to that place, and yet these places—London, Rome, Japan, China, North Korea, Mexico, Spain, Brazil, Morocco, Jerusalem—are more a part of me than the churches in Bandra that I visit or the cottages in and around my neighborhood, Bandra West.

My school library, Mrs. Ratnaswami, and Aruna's dusting mean more to me than these written words can ever express. I sometimes still catch myself wanting to dip my right index finger in boiling tea just so that I can feel one with a librarian whose library was a refuge to me.

"Pizza! You are impossible! Stop hiding behind bookshelves and come into the light!" I can hear her accusation and challenge to this day.

And no, I've not yet learned to come into the light.

crossword, bandra west

rossword is the most famous chain of bookshops in Mumbai, and they had an outlet on my turf in Bandra. Luckily for me, they moved even closer by the time I graduated from school and entered college.

The older shop had its outlet on the busy street on Linking Road. But in May 2005, the franchise bought a one-storied building, and a new Crossword outlet came into being.

It was a place I often had coffee and a chocolate cake thanks to the café attached to it on the first floor. I bought and read most of my books from that store including old favorites like the entire collection of Roald Dahl's children's books and something fresh, like all the latest Wilbur Smith paperbacks that I was quite addicted to fresh out of school.

I attended college at an institution nearby called St. Andrews College, which did not offer the subjects I wanted but had a great library and since no BSS student was attending it, I took the plunge and enrolled for the Arts course.

I would graduate in history and sociology after a rather peaceful study course of five years.

By 2005 Bandra West had rid itself of its pigs and kept only the dead ones sold at the pork shop on Bazaar Road. The Christian village look had disappeared over the years, and now a lot of non-Catholic residents populated the place, especially in the new towers and high-rise buildings built where old nineteenth- and early twentieth-century British cottages used to stand.

It was in such a climate of change that I visited Crossword, Bandra, every alternate day. I used to browse through the books, especially the thrillers. It was difficult to afford the books with the two thousand I was earning from giving tuitions. But the place was the hub of all rich and affluent Bandra West book lovers back then.

The Lotus bookshop had shut down, so every book lover went to Crossword. It was at Crossword that I bought my first autobiography of a contemporary politician, *Daughter of the East* by Benazir Bhutto.

I realized that there were a lot of other books written about politics, gender diversity, identity politics, and other current affair issues I wasn't aware of. I started taking on more students to tutor and saving up birthday, Christmas, and Easter cash for books related to contemporary issues.

Coffee and cafés were the fare of the day, and the café at Crossword, Bandra, was packed with affluent intellectuals whose conversations I listened to under the pretext of sitting down for coffee or hot chocolate. I heard many things that really shocked me. Me, the simpleton Catholic teenager of the early 2000s who wanted nothing more than to read and study literature in the degree college—later on I would focus on history and library sciences and the Indian National Movement for independence and sociology, where I specialized in gender studies and theories of the old and new school sociologists and postmodern thinkers.

All this was because of the education that I was receiving not only at my awesome college but also at Crossword Bandra, on Turner Road, the road of shoppers and famous jewelers. I still can't afford the jewelry, but I can afford a lot of books these days, and that's a comfort.

Never would I talk to the people at Crossword. Never would I forget the stuff about feminism, gender politics, and political scams they indirectly taught me.

Today, the place is not the same. No more intellectuals but a lot of children and teenagers looking for their vampire or Harry Potter book fix.

I still go there once in a while. The watchman with the pepper salt thinning mustache has been there since 2005, and he knows me well.

"Come after a long-time madamji. You must come more often," he says, as he the ever professional, opens the door for me. He used to call me "baba." That has since switched to "madam," and it makes me feel sad that it has to be so in life.

I was sixteen when I first bought my Wilbur Smith omnibus.

Now I'm twenty-nine, running my own tutorial, the director of a niche publishing firm and a writer.

Madam.

I come here for the Penguin red classics and some Indian fiction for my younger maternal aunt, whom I call Rita without the prefix or suffix of *aunty*. Even the floor boards seem at times to call out to me as I sit at my usual corner in the bookshop café and have a slice of cake with a soda.

It was here that I studied not only new ideas but also the mannerisms of people and their body language. They would soon appear in my short parable-like stories printed in the Catholic magazines and college magazines.

At the BSS school library, I was a loner whose body, heart, mind, and soul were focused only on the fiction I was reading. In the past, the only two people I used to observe were Mrs. Ratnaswami and Aruna. Here at Crossword, Bandra, I found the people that would appear in my fiction for a long time to come. Yes, I should come here more often. It always feels nice to be in a bookshop.

I traveled all around Bandra West through my term at college. I used to look for places where books could be found, and I always found them. I realized that Bandra West was a hub of readers and secondhand or lending libraries could be found nested in quiet corners where you would not likely expect them to be.

I didn't care for any place that did not sell what I wanted and craved for most in the world: books.

Half of my tuition money was banked and the other half I spent on books. I was thrifty. I am trying to remain so now. It's difficult, but I can do anything for books.

Crossword, Bandra, like my school library, was a fortress, especially during the rains and storms that seemed to shake our city of Mumbai in the latter part of the first decade. Whenever I could not get a rickshaw to head home, I would wrap my dark blue windcheater around me and row my way in my black boots to Crossword—or any other bookstore or lending library nearby college.

For most of us, Bandra West is still home, a place where the Christian minority can feel safe. But things are changing now.

Religious fundamentalism has reared its serpent head to pierce us with its venom of lies. They have already struck bookstores, putting books about spiritualism where books on physics should have been and placing books about plastic surgery in the Vedic times where hard-core medicine books used to be.

The political section is dwindling and a new form of history book is being placed on bookshelves where they have no right to be.

What's happening? Where is freedom of expression via the written word gone? Is it going to get worse?

Hindu—Muslim—Christian—Hindu—Muslim—Christian—Hindu—Hindu—HINDU!

The more I see, the more wary I grow. I feel helpless, like I did when my father used to come home to visit my mama. He was overbearing and too curt with our feelings. I hated his visits and the way he used to harp on how I was *his child* and he was *my father,* and so I should spend some quality time with *my dear papa!*

I loathed the man. But my mama loved him. Since they were not separated officially, had never filed for divorce under the Indian Marriage Act, he believed he had a right to visit. I hated him and his verbal tussles with Mama. How he used to make everyone feel uncomfortable. And how he used to call us on the phone at odd times and I was forced to speak to him.

"Fiza beta, Fiza beta, tell Mama to come back to me no ...

"I'm lonely Fiza beta, tell Mama to come back to me ...

"Fiza... beta.... you love Papa no ...

"Fiza beta ..."

I was the scapegoat for their tug-of-war game right through college, and sometimes even now. The man is intolerable. He resembles despots that surround me and the places that I once thought could always be free from them, bookshops and libraries, where the Word resides—my real father.

Hindu—Muslim—Christian—Hindu—Muslim—Christian—Hindu—Hindu—HINDU!

st. paul's books and art centre

Another place I started visiting while I was at degree college was the famous St. Paul's Bookshop in Bandra, which is run by the Pauline family under the guidance of the rules laid down by Blessed Alberione, who wished to spread God's word through media and books.

It had a Nun outlet and a Priest outlet, all a hop, skip, and a jump away from each other, and I used to visit them often with my godmother and elder maternal aunt, whom I call "Meshu," whose actual name is Mercia. No prefix or suffix of Godmother here either, and she remains even at age seventy my closest friend and confidant.

We've had the best of adventures together. She has taught me everything I've ever known about Christianity right from the time I was a toddler on my potty. I loved reading the children's Bible on the potty, I'll tell you that.

Seeing that I was so fascinated with books even at college and especially books about Christianity and the history of the Catholic Church, Meshu thought it best to introduce me to the Pauline society. She did so one summer's day, after I had visited Mt. Mary's Basilica with her for a prayer session.

She took me both to the one run by the priests on Turner Road and the one run by the nuns on Waterfield Road, both in Bandra West, and just a road apart from each other.

Both the stores were stocked with all sorts of Christian curiosities, from holy statues to Christian greeting cards to priests' silver chains, gold Jesus and Mary pens, prayer bookmarks, golden tabernacles, priests' vestments, Christian magnets, Christian holy water from Jerusalem, and mementos for baptisms, communions, silver jubilee marriages, twenty-first birthdays as well as framed and unframed images of Jesus, Mary, Joseph and the rest of the angels and the saints. And of course, books, books, and more BOOKS!

"Go around, dolly girl, and pick whatever you like and I'll pay," said my innocent Meshu very glad that I was fascinated by the place and that I wanted to browse.

We spent at one go almost ₹3,500 that day. I don't think Meshu even had money to go back to her home in Malad West. She had to borrow the money from Mama.

But I was so pleased with my purchases that the Pauline bookshops became my destinations to visit whenever anything new came in the books section. It has deepened the Christianity I know, but it also did something else that almost broke our family: it gave me a vocation. I wanted to become a nun.

"It's all because of you that such a pretty girl wants to waste the prime of her youth praying," my Mama would yell at Meshu when she saw the change that had come over me in a span of a year of visiting the Pauline bookshops.

Everyone was blaming Meshu for getting me involved with religion. Yes, now I supposedly had a vocation! The only child of my mama and the only offspring of my maternal family.

Everyone was more than a little upset. They were distraught.

I continued to read.

I slaved over books on religion, especially the Catholic religion for two years at a stretch. I read the Bible to glory and tried to learn Bible verses by heart or verbatim.

I read about the lives of different saints and poured over their writings too. Some of my favorites even today are St. Francis of Assisi, St. Catherine of Siena, St. Theresa of Avila, St. Claire, St. Don Bosco, St. Dominic Savio, St. John of the Cross, St. Alphonso Liguori, and St. Augustine. My favorite section in the store was the Tan book section, which brought out several rare Christian intellectual books every month. There was so much spiritual material to read and so little time, for I had a plan.

I had decided to join the convent by age eighteen or twenty. Not just any convent, but a cloistered convent, most preferably a Franciscan order.

I wanted to devote my time to prayer, contemplation, and reading the words of the holy ones.

"Why don't you lock yourself in our common bedroom if that's all there is to this madness of yours!" screamed my exasperated mama when I informed her of my plan and then read a page from St. Faustina's Diary.

Everyone was against it. So were some of the priests we knew personally.

"She hasn't got a degree, and she is too young," was the common refrain. But I was adamant. And so from 2007 to 2009, I devoted myself to not only reading the "secular works," as I called them, but also a lot of religious-based literature. Visits to the Pauline bookshops continued along with other things like working at the good old St. Francis of Assisi Church as a Sunday school teacher and then as an active member of the Assisi youth group.

My overall demeanor remained as it was in school: shy, reserved, uncommunicative, and bookish. But because of my dedication to the study of Christianity, especially the Bible, I was chosen first as a Diocese youth head of Bandra West, then the female representative head for the whole Catholic youth of Mumbai. All the while, I was lost in some book or another. Teenagers and young adults found me terrible to be with and I don't blame them at all. I was incorrigible where it came to books. I still am.

The Pauline bookshops made me more dedicated to my faith. The nuns and priests working there warmed to me because of my clout at the church as a Catholic youth leader, and so they gave me discounts. In fact, the day they saw my name as a female representative youth head of Mumbai, I got several books at highly discounted prices.

I was so happy and prayed in thanksgiving to St. Francis of Assisi for all that I was going through. It was so wonderful to be a Catholic in Bandra West.

I never spent the money I used for tuition on the books I bought from the Pauline bookshops. They were funded by Meshu and sometimes my poor mama, and believe me I wiped her account clean with my purchases.

Going to the Pauline bookshops was like a pilgrimage for me. I always returned with something or another to develop a greater love for God.

Then one day I made a decision. I would forgive my father.

I came to this decision due to a pamphlet, I can't remember its title, but it touched me to such an extent that within that moment, the hatred and resentment I felt towards this man, my father, vanished and it hasn't returned since.

I went all the way to Byculla by taxi with Meshu, one of the few taxi rides I made in my life at that time. The year was 2007, and I was 18 years old.

My father ran his own stationery store for students from schools and colleges. When he saw me, he recognized my mother's face and his eyes, and called me to sit down on his broken revolving seat.

"What have you come for after all this time?" he asked looking at the bustling crown of burka and skull cap crowd of Muslims passing up and down the busy polluted Byculla bridge road.

In a voice that I realized resembled his, I said, "I'm come to forgive you for abandoning my mother and me. Especially me."

He looked at his light green beaded rosary that he held in his stubby fingers. He replied casually, "I didn't abandon you. You don't understand. You were not a boy and I ..." He coughed as a means for changing the subject. "What are you studying?"

"Arts."

"No, I mean which subject?"

I replied with even breath, formally.

"History."

I felt he wouldn't understand what I meant by sociology or psychology, which were the other subjects in my syllabus. Besides, I wanted to get away from him. I was claustrophobic in the dusty shop, full of pens, pencils, schoolbags, chalk. But he surprised me.

He said, "Ah, so that's why you are here. To rake up the past, since you study history."

"I didn't mean *our* history ..." I faltered. This was so like him. Making it sound like he was the victim and I the sinner. And what was my crime pray tell? That I was a girl child? That I had the XX chromosome he provided when he lay down with my mother. That was something beyond my control to change. But then I was reading meta-physical and religious literature. Maybe ...

He explained with a sigh. "Fiza beta, life you know is like a river. The river doesn't go straight to the sea. There are several detours and several ups, downs, lefts, and rights until it finally reaches its resting place, the all-encompassing sea. Take me as one of those downs and just for-get the whole business and go on, live, while I die for your mother every day."

As usual he was making it sound like it was me who was the culprit, me who spoiled his oh-so-perfect marriage. I didn't hate him anymore after that moment. I pitied him, a deluded old man!

"How is Phila?"

Phila was the name he called Mama.

"How is her diabetes? Is she taking her medicine regularly?"

I fought back my hot smoldering tears as I said, "She is fine papa. She is living."

He nodded and fiddled with his green beads.

"But I am only existing," I added.

Then I called out to Meshu and we left the shop. We crossed the road, hailed a rickety cab and went back to Bandra West. As I observed the Muslim homes we passed on the way, with the call for aazaan (prayer) ringing out from all the mosques, I wondered what my life would have been if I had grown up here in Muslim Byculla? I did not see a single bookshop anywhere. I'm glad I lived in Bandra West, and I don't mind being communal by saying so. I have the right. I've got Muslim and Christian blood coursing through my veins.

I visited the Pauline bookshops after that only sparingly. The meeting with my father made me realize how close I was to having been brought up a strict Sunni Muslim.

I now was clearly aware of my many identities, and how different I was both from my non-reading father and mama. Woman, Minority Indian, Christian, South Indian Christian, Middle Class

Christian, and so much more if I were to study my paternal side.

What are identities anyway? To an existentialist mind like mine, it's all nothing within something that wants to ultimately be nothing.

But how after wanting to be a nun, having a vocation did I come to this idea of existing, and taking things as it came my way.

Many things happened. Most of them yet again in the books that I read.

Let's just say that by the end of my last year of BA college, I was done with my vocation and was ready to explore more books and more places where one could find them.

Now my own books are sold at the Pauline bookshops. One of the salesmen remembers me from the time I used to visit the store in the latter half of the first decade of the twenty-first century. He always looks at me with eyes of respect and a sort of, what, pride? That I am what his books created.

I was there just a week ago. I wanted a statue of St. Jerome the patron of librarians for obvious reasons. He said that no one prays to St. Jerome anymore. I guess that again shows how awfully peculiar I am in my tastes. Well, to set the record straight, I want the statue as a remembrance of a vocation that was and what things could have been; because to be frank, I hardly even believe these days that there is a God.

I requested the salesman to remember me if such a statue does arrive and then pushed through the sliding doors and left.

The place has grown bigger; the Pauline family has grown richer.

Now it's a huge complex with a Media college and houses on its ground floor a boutique bookstore which was where I wrote my first novella in longhand.

The complex is now referred to as the St. Paul's Institute of Communication Education, Bandra West, and is well known throughout the suburbs. Many students flock to it. It's beautiful and massive, the pride and joy of Bandra West. And I was there when the new complex was inaugurated. Meshu and I purchased booklets and statues of the Last Supper, and I wondered what could have been if I had really joined that cloister convent of mine.

Jesus Christ!

title waves boutique bookstore

More than anything else I wanted to be a writer.

So, with the go ahead, Blaise managed to publish my very first book on Amazon CreateSpace back in 2012.

It was called *S.O.S Animals and Other Stories* with parable-like Christian stories that I was planning to serialize in a Catholic newsletter at that time. Most of my writing was highly Christian in many ways, and so I was regularly published in Catholic magazines as a youth contributor.

When the newsletter that promised to publish my stories refused to do so, after only publishing one story 'Animal Mass' from the book, Blaise published the book on Amazon.

It was not a success, but at the time I'd decided to concentrate on building my own tutorial to fund my writing and the family expenses.

It was 2012, and I had no place in my house nor peace in the house with its three pokey rooms with pealing wall paint where you could hear a sneeze right from the second floor to the ground floor, where five of us resided. I needed a place to write. Back then, I was still writing in longhand, just like my mentor Ruskin Bond. But I really needed a place, which also had a clean toilet, to write in.

In came the new boutique store which was housed on the ground floor of the St. Paul's Institute of Communication. It's called "Title Waves." It wasn't like my school library, but it had a clean café attached to it. I decided to write there.

I used to park myself there from its opening at 10:00 a.m. until 4:00 p.m. without lunch, since I couldn't afford it and because I couldn't waste time going home and coming back to Title Waves for something as trivial, in my mind, as nonliterary as lunch!

I would write after ordering a cappuccino or a café mocha or some Earl Grey or English Breakfast tea and then scratch – scratch – scratch the whole morning and afternoon away until I really had to go back to take tuitions, which went right up to 8:00 p.m. or sometimes 9:00 p.m., if I was taking a senior student, and then I would spend the latter half of my wee hours reading.

The books at Title Waves were amazing but with my tuition fees I really couldn't afford to buy much. I used to roam their wonderful aisles, with polished flooring smelling of lemongrass and grandly displayed bookshelves with all sorts of books, especially a wonderful selection of books on science, philosophy, history, and politics.

It took some time after the store was set up for it to catch a really big crowd, but today it's the most active and happening place in Bandra West for literary events. Everyone seems to want to have their book launch at Title Waves. My own books are sold there now, but I still remember those days when I used to chug down cappuccino after cappuccino as I wrote a new set of parable short stories and my very first novella called *Nirmala: The Mud Blossom.*

Just like at Crossword Bandra, I wrote, but I also watched the different types of people that came to the bookstore as well as the café for a hot or mostly cold coffee.

I learned what a waffle was and how one was supposed to eat the damn messy thing by observing others. I used to see many Bollywood actors and actresses entering and leaving the place, including well-known and worshiped celebrities like Saif Ali Khan, Kareena Kapoor Khan, Shahid Kapoor, Arbaaz Khan, and many others whom I know from sight but not by name.

I guess I used to see a lot of Saif and Kareena because they stayed very close to the store and got their fix of books there. Saif was quite a reader, always browsing through international titles, usually in a pair of running shorts that showed off his gorilla-hairy legs, while Kareena was fond of reading books on food, cinema, and travel. She wore hardly any make up and a track suit. I presumed they hit the gym near the boutique often.

By the descriptions, dear reader, you must have put two and two together that this area was one of the posh parts of Bandra West, and you could not have been more right about that. Besides, with the arrival and departure of so many media people, the place caught on and teenagers with their slang and short shorts, came to the café to hang out with their friends. I observed and wrote.

The book *Nirmala* was finished in two weeks' time, after which I went on to write its stand-

alone sequel *Amina: The Silent One,* in another curated library-cum-bookstore, but more of that in
another bookish essay.

I saw luxurious living. I saw the youngsters of
the present day with their Justin Bieber faces and
Zayn Malik tuft of dirty blonde hair, and I was
more intrigued than fascinated. Times were
changing, and I would have to keep up with the
times but in my own unique way, by writing
about the things that really mean something to
me.

Nirmala was not my best work, but critics
loved it, and I won a bunch of indie awards for it.
Nirmala was about a girl who was hated because
she was, well, a girl.

Nirmala was a girl I would never have wanted
to be, but about whom I felt most comfortable
writing about.

You see, that could have been me for all I
know.

My family members, even after twenty-nine
years, have not been open about why my father
didn't want a girl child, nor why his parents refused to look after me because I was a girl.
Further, they have never explained how or why
it was apparently dangerous for my parents to
leave me, a babe in arms, alone with my relatives,

including my own paternal grandmother, whom everyone thought to be a witch, in my father's home.

All I know is that one day when I was three months old, my parents went to work and left me at my father's home. I don't remember whether it was Mama or Papa who came back from work to find either my paternal aunt or uncle with their leg very near my tiny, delicate head. My nappy hadn't been changed for over ten hours, and I had developed a rash because of it. I think I hadn't been fed, either. My mama was sure that they were planning to drop me down the stairs if she went to work again the next day.

The deal was simple, you see.

My mama gave birth to a girl and that was the first mistake.

To atone for that mistake, she had to leave her lucrative teaching job at the prestigious BSS and become a housewife because none of my paternal aunts wanted to look after *a girl child*.

So the story goes, my mama refused, she came back to live with nana, and the case was shut with only a few visits from my father. I became a bookworm and wrote this essay about Title Waves, a rich and lavishly designed boutique bookshop, which is so very different from my actual history, the history of my life.

Nirmala's life.

Sometimes it's better to be lost in a book, either reading or writing it, isn't it?

I wrote my days away at Title Waves until I found other places to write and then rented my own office-cum-writing hut near my home. My business has grown, sort of. I'm still in my struggling years, but I can afford to taste the cappuccinos of all Mumbai, and nothing tastes similar to the brew at the café at Title Waves, where I gave birth to *Nirmala*.

I go to Title Waves often, sometimes to distribute my books, but more often to buy their awesome stationary and titles from their fiction section. Last week I bought seven books in the Indian fiction section for Rita, my aunt. I've got her hooked on reading. It took her sixty-six years to catch the reading bug.

I'm a happier bookworm, because I followed the principle, *The early book catches the worm and turns it into a "bookworm."*

mcubed library

I was a struggling teacher and writer in 2013 when I came across, on St. Andrews Road, Bandra West, a small but well-maintained library called the Mcubed Library, also known as the Maharashtra Mitra Mandal Library. It was recommended to me by a teacher colleague of mine.

Being the introvert and recluse I was and still am, I sent my aunt Mercia (Meshu) to check the place out for me. She found it to be clean and tidy, with a wonderful adult library section.

"How is the toilet?" I asked, keeping my fingers crossed. I needed to know because I planned to spend many hours there every day.

"It's an English toilet separate for women and is cleaned every morning at 10:30 a.m.," answered Meshu with a smile, looking at me over her horn-rimmed spectacles.

"Perfect," said I, and enrolled as a library member.

Compared to Title Waves and Crossword, the place is a much humbler setting and is situated on the ground floor of an apartment complex. It has two sections: a children's section and an adult section. I fell in love with it, especially its adult fiction and nonfiction section and the quietness of the place. They offer a membership for borrowing books. I took the one called "Galaxy," which entitled me to four books for a two-week period.

I settled in the next morning on a sofa chair in the adult section reading room and began to write, yet again in longhand, the first few couplets of my first poetry book *So This Is Love*. Two other rooms, along with a few nooks and comfortable corners, offered readers or students a place to sit quietly and read a book, newspaper, or magazine.

Two librarians oversaw the running of the place. They changed positions at 3:00 p.m. Books were plentiful, and the place itself was clean, neat, and not at all dusty. The shelves were dusted on a regular basis. It was also swept and swabbed on a regular basis with new books being inducted into the library on the first Wednesday of every month.

The place was dedicated to inspiring adults and children to read, and they allowed students, especially the poor, a clean place to study at an affordable price. Some of the Wadi boys from the hut tenement near my residence patronize the library on a regular basis.

If Mcubed taught me anything, well, it actually taught me a long list of things, but the first would have to be discipline.

Yes, I learned to return my books on the due date, and if I didn't, which these days I often do, I have to pay a fine. That would be ₹2 for one book per day not returned on time. That is affordable now, but back then it was outrageously extravagant, and for that reason I used to keep my dates.

The next thing I learned was about dedication. The poor college students who studied there were so dedicated to their textbooks that they would rarely look up from them.

Everyone at that time thought I was a student myself, when actually I was penning both of my poetry books. I used to take a rickshaw going and coming. That amounted to ₹20 in all spent. This was 2013, and back in 2009, before the rickshaw hike in fare, the total would have amounted to ₹16. I was counting each and every rupee back then, especially when I thought that some of these OBC/ST/SC students couldn't even afford the "Star" membership, which included one single book for only ₹1,000 a year.

Like the time I spent at Title Waves, I never went back home for lunch. But I would take tea, and some of the lads there used to share their desserts. I used to have my tea like Ruskin Bond, one of my favorite writers, with lots of sugar and milky.

I learned about a book club that met once every month. I attended a few sessions but couldn't start a conversation because of my shyness. But I really loved the women I met there, especially one who would later become a friend of mine. To this day, I see her regularly at the library and I've spoken to her quite often. Unfortunately, I've never remembered her name … I am absentminded quite a bit!

Mcubed Library is somber until a children's event is going on; then there is a ruckus that even the most studious of readers and writers cannot ignore. But give me the laughter of little children any day compared to the sound of that television and adult Maharashtrian men playing cricket!

If I was somber earlier in my life, I think I became even more solemn and solitary at Mcubed Library. It's a cozy place, and a hub for local activities, thanks to the people who run the establishment.

If I had time, I would certainly have attended their monthly movie sessions for adults, where they screen movies based or adapted from books.

Being a part of their activities and their work to help the unfortunate produces a community feeling. I like how they've supported Bandra West, which has a very avid reading population, and made it even richer bookwise.

I remember that I read nonfiction for most of a year at Mcubed. I read books that were close to my work and my mission as a teacher and writer, as well as anything that sounded superb and whose cover was ancient.

I have read most of the rare biographies and autobiographies at Mcubed, including writings of India's self-publishing industry, which are not always registered on Goodreads.

In this regard I've read many books that have been beautifully written but have not caught on with the readers, or let's say the sort of readers that make popular books popular. I loved reading

Mcubed Library's Indian short story collections. They are gems and a pleasure to read.

Later, when my tutorial started to pick up a bit, I started going to Mcubed only on weekends to write a few sketches or essays in my personal diaries, as I was booked for teaching all through the week. At times, due to late night research for the books I was to write later, I managed only to sleep at 8:00 a.m. on weekdays and get up at 2:30 p.m., just in time for class.

I would not get an opportunity to sit at Mcubed because all the available chairs, sofas, etc. were full of readers, writers, and young students; they are that popular as a public library and reading community in Bandra West.

I now go to Mcubed only on occasion, as I've no need to sit there anymore, thanks to having rented my own office-cum-writing hut.

In 2016, just before I moved into my office, I continued to visit Mcubed, mainly because of its old-world charm as a disciplined and old-fashioned library. I read all the rare copies and editions of Ruskin Bond books there. Ruskin Bond, in my mind, can be clearly associated with everything that Mcubed stands for, as I read and reread most of his early works there.

I'm still struggling with my career, or careers, I should say. I'm juggling it all, and I don't know how I get up and when I go to bed. That's why being part of a library is so important for me, and that is why I keep renewing my Mcubed Library yearly membership. It's important for a book phoenix (that's what my students call me these days) like me to know that whatever dips occur in business, there will always be an affordable library near home for me to go to whenever I wish.

I think it is the comforting aura that has made Mcubed a place where even Bollywood celebrities and high society people flock to, especially with their children, to encourage them to read and keep to their due dates.

Once when I was writing one of my diary entries on one of the sofa chairs in the adult library section, who should walk in but Bollywood's star mom and wife, Aamir Khan's wife Kiran Rao with their two-year-old son. She, a millionaire, was sifting through the shelves trying to find something to read while at the same time talking in a lilting tender voice to her son.

She smiled at me as she made her choice from the international-fiction section and walked out.

All Bandra West mothers bring their brood of children to Mcubed, most of the educated parents at least. My own history professor patronizes the library with her two adorable children, and she says that many of the Andrew's College crowd does the same. I wouldn't know. I'm not good with crowds.

It's October 2018 as I type this essay in my office-cum-writing hut, not far from Bandra West's elite Bandstand society. Diwali, the Hindu festival of lights, will soon be upon us, and Mcubed is bound to have some event to participate in as a community.

I'll check which days the festivities are taking place, and then visit the library on other days when I can be left alone, with a Ruskin Bond book by my side.

10

my college library: st. andrews

The only thing I wanted in a college I wanted to study in after school was that it should not be filled with students from BSS; it should be in Bandra West because I did not want to travel far; it must have a good library.

St. Andrews College of Arts, Commerce, and Science met all my criteria, especially the last one.

The college is young compared to the church it is attached to, which of course is St. Andrews Church—the oldest heritage church in Bandra West. The college was established in the 1980s and has, with sheer dint and effort, now become an A-grade college of highest esteem.

I loved my college. I loved the way it protected me just the way my school library protected me. There was no Mrs. Ratnaswami or ever dutiful Aruna here, but the library at St. Andrews was my refuge for all five years I studied there.

There was enough room to house books and students alike. The head librarian was strict and a tough disciplinarian whose voice boomed every time she opened her mouth to speak.

The library was stocked with books of every category and every genre. Attendance at classes was compulsory and when I was not studying and taking down lecture notes at class, well, I was reading in the library.

That library changed a lot about what I stood for in life.

My initial goal upon entering college was to study English literature and major in it. I had been reading only fiction books all my school life in the presence of Mrs. Ratnaswami and Aruna. I was a hard-core Dickens girl. I wanted to teach litera-ture for money to buy books to read and food to eat.

"Pizza! You are reading fat-fat Dickens in dark light. Please read biographies too!" Mrs. Ratnaswami would order me as she switched on the lights and fans around the place I was sitting.

I have never, without compulsion, listened to the advice of elders so throughout my school life I did not take her sound advice to delve into nonfiction and see the real world.

At Andrews, I finally was compelled to, and I'm glad about it.

The college was like a school really. All the professors knew all the students by name and the principal as well as the dean were always on their rounds so nobody really got into mischief.

We were well protected and got enough notes to help even a dunce pass an exam with a first class. It was a radiant, teenager and young adult–friendly atmosphere, with every comfort a student could want.

I loved my college. I loved the way everyone let me alone and allowed me to stay in the library alone for hours to read, pen notes, and research.

I studied English, Hindi, psychology, history, economics, sociology, and advertising in the beginning. Each time I passed through the two large floors of our library in search of books for study, I became overwhelmed.

I found my true self then. I realized that there was more to this world than Little Nell's death and Uriah Heap's treachery. There was so much to the gamut of living in this world. You know, being a woman, then maybe being a feminist, then being part of a caste hierarchy that indulged in caste politics, then the impoverishment of the poor, the ideals of socialism vs. communism, regionalism, urban vs. rural identities, population studies, health issues, the rise of dysfunction in most of the institutions in existence, dowry debts, farmer debts, bride burning, female infanticide, female feticide, politics and power rather than service, the fall of the rupee, racism, identity politics, gender diversity. ... All this and much more became a part of me as I took down book after book from the metal-and-glass shelves and brought them to my well-lit corner of the library.

The books opened my eyes to realities that only a good library can.

I felt pain, sorrow, regret, and compassion all at the same time as I poured over volumes of text, most of them first editions and very neatly kept good clean copies.

I started reading Hindi novels, short story collections, and nonfiction books. I grew to love the Hindi language and stood first in. I received a lot of scholarship money because of my excellence in the subject. My favorite professor was Manish sir, who was a master at his craft. Oddly, to date, he doesn't know my name; just my roll number, 116, and that is what the dear man calls me.

It often is the case that it's the people who make up the places that really influence our lives. That's how it was with my professors at Andrews. They educated me and loved me, and I will always remember them fondly.

Both my mama and papa had only been school graduates. It seems my papa joined college but dropped out in less than a year because he had to take over the family business of selling stationary goods from his diabetic father, my paternal grandfather, yet another man I've never known. Everyone insists that my behavior and certain mannerisms are just like his.

My paternal grandfather's name was Ibrahim. He had never been to school but was very bright, apparently. I was taken to see him when he lay on his death bed in the latter part of the 1990s.

It was one of his last wishes—to see me, his first-born son's only child. Technically speaking, I was the first claimant to the property. But, alas, I was estranged, and all through the meeting Mama and Papa were fighting, throwing verbal barbs of poison at each other while I stood at Ibrahim's deathbed, wondering why I had been brought to see someone who didn't even know that I would rather be happier at home with a book.

All these old faded memories, like a faded black-and-white photograph, came back to me as I read books in the college library, whose foundation stone was laid by none other than Mother Teresa herself. I thought to myself as I studied about new theories in philosophy, social studies, et al., that I was almost apparently like one of the girls I was reading and studying about.

Luckily for the deliverance of Nana, there would have gone I. ...

I loved reading fiction all the same. I loved to pick up a new fiction title from the English literature section of the library.

I met in its shelves most of the writers and poets I would later emulate in my writings: J. D. Salinger, Emile Zola, John Irving, Salman Rushdie, Rohinton Mistry, James Joyce, Philip Larkin, Milan Kundera, Maxim Gorky, Chitra Banerjee Divakaruni, F. Scott Fitzgerald, Charles Lamb, D. H. Lawrence, William Faulkner, and more.

The library opened earlier than the college, and I was always the first to walk in with my sling bag and faded black jeans. I would deposit the bag in a slot near the counter and pick out the material I needed for study, then pick up a newspaper to read, either the *DNA* or the *Indian Express*, and then sit down to read. If tea was distributed, I would have some but very rarely. I was always too engrossed in what I was doing to care about tea.

By the time I had to specialize, I took history and sociology as my double major. Everyone at home was not pleased.

"You're not taking English literature! You must be mad! After all that reading indeed. ... "

"History will pull down your percentage. Take English instead."

"Major in English. You've got the talent, girl. Think again!"

"Why don't you become a law graduate? You always seem to be buried in you books anyway?"

"But sociology is not a paying subject. You're acting mad. Take psychology instead."

"Sociology is an okay-okay subject. Psychology will make people's heads turn!"

But I stuck to my resolve. I, a writer and English teacher today by profession, took history and sociology as my graduation subjects, and I have never regretted it.

I was keen on studying history as well as sociology because more than anything else, they were very revealing and interesting for my hungry brain.

Today, my publishing company has the imprint *Freedom with Pluralism.* We focus on publishing quality work that is based on social issues, education, and the benefit of all. I don't think all this would have happened if I had stuck only with English literature throughout my education. My education would have been incomplete.

If Andrews did anything more significant for me than educating me, it was to make me love to study, take down lecture notes and love to learn new things and have loads to study more along the way. It was a place fertile for a bookish armchair intellectual. I remain in its debt.

If I wasn't in the library, then I was at the Andrews chapel either contemplating my future or reading the Bible. Most of the crowd at Andrews were Christians and so the chapel was visited regularly, especially every time a student entered the premises and left for the train station or the main road to head home.

So, the place was always bubbling over with people. I didn't like company, but I guess one has to tolerate.

And living in harmony with everyone and anyone is what Andrews stood for. All the Christian institutions here in Bandra West try to inculcate that maxim in the minds of all its students, teachers, and workers.

Things are changing though. It's changing subtly, but it's changing all right.

But Andrews still seems to be out of the regular fanatical crowd, for now.

It has always opened its doors to those who have yearned to educate themselves and make something decent of themselves.

Its stone walls have nurtured, cherished, and blessed its alumni. I hope to do it proud someday by returning to my studies and finishing my masters, at least.

The walls of the college library are a witness to my days of study and reading. Let's hope that those memories remain and more students enter this humble institution with nothing and leave with a little more than just a degree.

books, places, identity, personality

What kind of rigid identity or personality would you expect me to have when most of my waking hours have been spent reading various kinds of books?

They say one who reads books leads many lives while one who doesn't leads only one life.

Through the books in my home, school, college, bookshops, and lending libraries, I have traveled to many a place real and unreal, back in time, and far ahead into many versions of our future. And all that it has required is a book or Kindle in my hand.

I come back, therefore, to the beginning. A person who has read as avidly, sincerely, and voraciously as me cannot be expected to have a rigid set identity, personality, or overall feelings toward any particular place. In fact, what are places in the world of a reader and writer who goes to only a few libraries and bookshops, but through their time machines (books) have traveled the cosmos—past, present, and future?

I therefore am aware of the fact that I do not have a fixed personality. It changes as rapidly as the turning of the page of a fast and racy thriller; yet it seems still and simple because most of the time that I am awake I am silently reading the printed page. I speak very little vocally. Most of my *speaking* is done through the written word or through my teaching. I'm moody by nature, but I've overcome that fault through the rigorous schedule of reading at least three hours in a day.

I don't know anything at all about my paternal heritage—nor the family members involved and their personalities. No one seems inclined to tell me anything about it.

"I don't go back to the past," is my mama's prepared answer for anything Papa related. At the rate it's going, I don't think I'll ever know anything about the characteristics that have been passed to me genetically and places that must or could have shaped my personality on that side of the family.

Jesus, I don't even know which part of India my father is from!

And that's a really hard thing to say because aside from orphans, everybody in India knows where they are from. I once joked with my students that I came from Afghanistan, but they said Afghans are supposed to be pretty and very tall, and so I changed the topic, going on with the lesson for that day.

I've really not traveled at all. Never been out of the country. Never wanted to. Such a waste of precious literary time, don't you think?

I've really only been to Bangalore and Mysore and Lonavala.

Blaise apparently did buy a vacation house in Pune but now someone else is staying in it and refuses to get out, so we've never been to Pune either! I would have loved Pune only because it is land locked. The further I am from that dreadful Arabian Sea, the happier I am about the safety of my books.

So, yes, I'm not a firm personality of sorts. I go by the title existentialist, but that basically means I could just be anything–Catholic, Muslim, Hindu, my driver, the man in the moon, J. K. Rowling (oh, I wish), Putin, the gingerbread man, a Republican, my cat Trotskyna, my other cat Lopez, their mate Band. ... They're in a polyamorous relationship with a neighboring cat called Kekobad. Kekobad tags along with Band's estranged twin brother Speckled (Speckled Band ... remember Sherlock Holmes?) ... *What the hell am I doing?* Well, basically that means I can be anything at any time.

Books are my life. If I was a man, books would have been my wife.

Where I find books, there I go.

Where I can write more books, there I remain.

In the middle of all this chaos is my garden, which I tend to; music, which I occasionally listen to on my Bose speaker; and aromatic therapy, which helps me with a breathing problem. I have severe sleep apnea.

So, not many new places and almost the same reflections from and on them but still, I live because of them and am still a part of society; I think.

My cats go to more interesting places which you could write any number of fat tomes about. I love cats, can't stand snakes, and feel a bit faint when I see a scorpion. I run in panic when I see anything with more than thirty-three legs–does that sound like somebody you know?

Then again, with all that religious stuff I was and still am reading, I think I've learned to believe that wherever we go and whatever we do, someone somewhere is feeling and doing the very damn same thing, so what the hell?!

There are too many exclamation marks in this essay. And I have read in some writer's guide that there should be very few exclamation marks in an essay. But then, how many of us can maintain that all our lives? We either act like "full stops," where every place makes us feel the same whatever the circumstance. Or else we live like everyone does, like exclamation marks, wishing every time there is something new to do and a new place to go, even if it is through the pages of a good paperback on your night stand.

Right now, I'm sitting in my office-cum-writing-hut near my home.

The place is crowded with books. There are curios that help me when I have nothing to write about. The statue of St. Francis of Assisi is watching my back as I write, and for the love of God I hope one day he doesn't start talking to me. I hate Gods who talk; they are better off quiet as the grave.

I prefer the sound of my make shift St. Francis of Assisi fountain in front of me, with rivulets of water falling and making gushing sounds that remind me of Ruskin Bond's little brook, which ultimately leads him to the main river, the one he knew would take him to the sea.

Sea—river—Papa—my father.

I've never known you father. I don't even think that day is ever going to come.

You never read. Mama doesn't read. Then where do these words come from? If it is not from the places, the bookshops, and the libraries I've visited then where else?

So, you could say I have become who I am because of the places I've been, because no one in my maternal family is like me. And I will never know anything about Papa and his family.

Because he wanted a *boy*.

trilogy

It was the year 2015. I had completed my stint as a substitute teacher at BSS. It was now April, and the exams were over. I was doing well but still needed a better place to go to write in peace.

That's when Blaise pointed out a newspaper article in a weekend issue. It spoke about a curated library-cum-bookshop for book lovers established in 2014 by a young married couple. The article said that the place was quiet: the perfect place to write a story.

We found our way with great difficulty. Thank goodness for our private cab driver. He is our man Friday and devoted to driving me wherever I want to head out to. Yes, I was starting to get on a bit well by then.

So, we found the place in town, at Lower Parel, or Bombay town area, as the taxi drivers are prone to call it. It was in one of the interior parts of the old British Parel mill area. Now it was a shopping complex near one of Mumbai's largest shopping malls, Phoenix Mills.

Called Trilogy: The Eternal Library, it was, and still is, one of the most peaceful libraries I've ever been to. One patron beautifully described the place as a library-cum-bookshop where the loudest sound you could basically hear was the turning of pages.

Bliss!

I wrote there for the whole of April and May. I went there alone with my driver. He used to park himself down in the parking lot while I climbed the stairs to the first floor and sat on a comfortable cushioned chair opposite a fantastic view of an ancient peepul tree overlooking the Jewish graveyard of Worli.

I wrote in a diary about a girl child with a talent for music.

It became my highly acclaimed novel *Amina: The Silent One.*

It is a stand-alone sequel to *Nirmala: The Mud Blossom.* I wrote continuously from 10:30 a.m. to 1:00 p.m., after which I went back home to prepare to teach classes for children ranging from grades five to ten.

I came back every morning of April and May and wrote at least 2,000 longhand words per day, weekends excluded.

I took ginger milk tea with a lot of sugar biscuits while writing the novel, all courtesy of the wonderful owners, the young couple spoken of earlier, Ahalia and Meethil, the wife and husband duo. I was spoiled silly by them.

I wrote many books, essays, short stories, articles, and novels at Trilogy, until I rented out my office-cum-writing hut near home. It saves time and I can have regular meals, which are a necessity now because of acute acidity and digestive problems I developed due to my wayward lifestyle and erratic eating habits of earlier years.

When I go there, to that beautiful library, I remember the pleasure of so many days of my latter twenties spent writing and reading at Trilogy. The smell of ginger tea reminds me of my Amina just like cappuccinos remind me of my Nirmala. These girls of mine don't have a face, but they do have a taste and a soothing smell, which until my last days I shall never forget.

Like my other writings, studying and reading haunts it's like a fortress with security cameras all around. Trilogy means I've come home to the many stories that are more real to me than my own identity, my own personality, my background, and my murky past.

I identify Trilogy with books, ballpoint ink smells, and contemplation.

I've contemplated a lot upon my life sitting at Trilogy. I've made decisions very crucial to my present state in that very place. And I will never forget the beautiful books, especially collector editions, I read and purchased there.

I've discovered wonderful titles, small publishing firms, and rare collections at Trilogy. But most of all, I associate the place with peace, contentment, and where dreams were dreamed and wishes suddenly fulfilled.

I learned to talk at last there.

They started holding a book club for all members. Ahalia, the curly-haired, South Indian beauty with brains made it possible for some of us to meet once a month to discuss books that we had read or were planning to read. *Discuss* meant that I would have to speak. I was so nervous about it, I'm not the speaking type at all. Where some writers have the gift of the gab, I didn't even have a set voice of my own.

But I managed. Somehow. Shaky at the beginning, but then when I started talking about the books I loved and had read, the speaking part of it went pretty well.

No one at the club thought that I could have a communication problem. I made friends. I spoke and was spoken to. The feeling was good and I hope the feelings were mutual.

Ahalia had this unique way of running the book club topics by not choosing a book to read in particular but a topic or genre that we could read over the month in fiction or nonfiction. Some examples were travel, history, historical structure, and science.

We had a lot of fun at these meetings. Two good friends I made at the club were Kanchana and Sravya. I am no longer in touch with Sravya, as she has moved to the United States to study virology. I've grown very close to Kanchana, and yet I've not told her all of my secrets.

I have many secrets, which I wish to keep within me until my death.

It's all in my personal diaries, which after my death I wish to be published for a certain cause.

It's strange to talk about death when writing about as fascinating, vibrant, and soothing a place as Trilogy. But think, because of its soothing and balm-like nature, I have managed to heal old wounds that festered for quite a long time.

I've learned to accept melancholy as part of my overall bearing.

My father was melancholic too. Always sad that he was not allowed to actually do the things he wished to do, like finish college to become a doctor. He wanted to be a doctor. My father. My Papa; the only personal detail he shared with me.

*I have walked through the many pages of your
library,
I have sung and danced as I have held to my heart
your books;
I have placed my memories in every corner of this
place of tomes,
And I'll be reading here even when you've gone.*

Glass walls surround the whole of Trilogy. The sunlight plays hide-and-seek through its shelves, and birds like green parrots visit the bird feeder. I watch them as I write.

The place is air-conditioned so I am always at peace there bodily, especially because I am a person who is prone to perpetually feeling warm. Blaise most of the time, if not all the time, accompanies me to Trilogy. We have had a lot of quiet times there.

Blaise, my Godfather, my true father, who used to read stories like *Three Little Pigs*, *Hansel and Gretel* and *Snow White and the Seven Dwarfs* when I was a toddler in order to put me to sleep. Blaise, who tied my shoelaces when I couldn't, taught me to see the magic in books, and who is devoted to me as a father should be. He, too, is here most of the time with me at Trilogy, because I guess we have always been together in the places I love from the longest time that I can re-member.

And if the reincarnation theory is true, then maybe we've been together in many other places for far longer. I am in behavior more his daughter than my father's.

He likes Trilogy too. He loves to read and con-template there too.

At Trilogy, the rich people of Parel come along with college students. Many come with kinder-garten children, hoping to inspire them to read and love books. Events are held regularly, which makes the place important for bibliophiles in Worli. Meethil is a professional wildlife photog-rapher. So many photographers come and some display their work here. I have always had a fascination for wildlife and nature in general; I love the loamy soil I knead with my stubby small hands for the trees I plant and care for, my resilient Neem who always needs more space and my brave Drumstick, whose leaves are often chewed by Lopez the cat. My love for wildlife has been nurtured at Trilogy.

My plants keep on growing, and so will my love for my quiet space at Trilogy.

"I know that gesture," says Ahalia when she sees me entering the library section, then me rubbing the palms quickly with an impish smile on my face. That means I'm taking a lot of books this time as well.

Ahalia and Meethil understand my needs, and they keep me comfortable.

If only most people were like this, the world would not be in the mess it is in.

I love my journeys to and from Trilogy as much as I love spending time there. Trilogy is in a Dalit area that once was home to the writer I owe a lot to as a history student and as a nonfiction writer, Dr. B. R. Ambedkar, god and mentor to many. His statue stands at the center of the roads crisscrossing each other as my driver, Blaise, and I near Trilogy.

What would this leader of the masses, succor for the untouchables, have said in response to the problems and deplorable state his India, which he with others created for us, now find itself in?

Where confusion of ideals and barbarities beyond understanding are enacted, especially upon his own people, the Dalits, Gandhi's so called Hairjans?

I bow to him with respect every time I pass his home, the place where he walked and talked, and where he loved, cried, and occasionally laughed. I read a lot of his works from the small presses that Trilogy encourages by showcasing their work. Because of him, I learned how to write non-fiction.

My Ambedkar, my Babasaheb. Long live Babasaheb!

Trilogy has many stacks of books on the subject of feminism. They also have many books written about and by women. One day I bought the whole section and emptied their shelf. They are used to that by now. It wasn't the first time, and I hope it won't be the last.

But these feminism books, along with some books on my favorite topics like Dalit studies, the rise of the Naxalites, socialism, communism, and gender diversity, have continued my studies in an indirect manner.

I hope to be a postgraduate one day soon. I don't want to be interred in the soil without completing my education.

And yet, I have so many stories to write and so much teaching to do. When will I find the time? These thoughts and others cloud my mind as I peruse the shelves of Trilogy, especially on quiet mornings, as the sun pours through its many windows and the smell of my Amina, or ginger tea, fills the atmosphere. And then I feel that maybe some stories are meant not only to be read and written, but felt, like a beam of sunshine on your right gnarled palm that reeks of ink.

granth bookstore

The Granth Bookstore is strategically located on the boundary of Khar and Juhu, which some non-Mumbaikars still consider part of the Bandra West suburb. This is not true. Rather, it's NEAR THE SEA and is the hub of bookish activity in that part of the suburbs.

I go there often, ever since I hired my private taxi and the driver to take me there. Otherwise you wouldn't catch me dead near any sort of sea, sand, or anything else beachy.

I go there for its coffee table books, its books on cinema, its wonderfully kept stock, and because I love their cappuccinos.

I take my coffee with three lumps of sugar. I know it's unhealthy, but I don't care, better caffeinated liquid than that awful sea I have to abide by if I have to go there.

Blaise takes his coffee with two lumps of sugar and is always roaming around in their graphic fiction section or their religious section. Basically, all their sections are fantastic, and I would love to come here more often, but I just can't bear the sea.

Granth means *book*, and I associate this place with my new position in life as publisher and director of Fiza Pathan Publishing OPC Private Limited. I associate this place with the smell of well-covered books, vanilla extracts, cleanliness, and the elite. For the elite crowd shops here all the time. If you want to spot your favorite Bollywood, television, and Netflix stars of the screen, and you don't want to go to Bandstand, Bandra West, then spend some quality time reading a book here at Granth, and you'll see them popping in. They are more at ease here in their favorite bookshop than anywhere else, and you are more capable of having a conversation with them here than at a restobar or a studio.

I've seen quite a few in my time. But I don't approach them because I'm not good at conversations. I like Twinkle Khanna best. She is a Bollywood celebrity turned writer who writes really amazing books and is a book lover to the core. I love when the bookstore showcases the books that she recommends; I always buy the lot.

The staff here are very helpful and encouraging. But I prefer to be on my own. When I am there, attending their book launches and other events, I feel regal and full of energy with good vibes. Whenever I need to fuel myself for another hectic term of teaching or for another book I have to write, I come here.

I come here to remind myself that my writing has taken me to places I never thought I would go; yet, to be as simple as a Ruskin Bond collection of poems about nature.

The décor of the bookstore is magnificent, with money plants and sunflowers growing in re-cycled bottles that look so good you want to take them home with you. I spend hours here, reading the books I've bought and sipping cups and cups of cappuccinos with Blaise.

The famous Juhu beach is nearby and there-fore this road is always crowded, especially on Saturdays, which is when I manage to come here.

I sometimes write in my diary here. The place inspires me to do so.

The road otherwise is full of designer shops and boutiques for Indian wedding dresses. Mama rarely comes here with me. She feels out of place among the rich and glamorous, while I have no problem just being myself.

Mama, for whom I buy coffee table books with photographs of the legendary Bollywood actor of actors Amitabh Bachchan. He is her favorite actor and luckily for her she has met him several times in person. This was so because she taught his kids back in the 1980s, at BSS, when they were small. He may have forgotten her, my young dazzlingly beautiful Mama, but she has never forgotten him. It has been her pleasure to have been so close to his life in a small way.

We at home call him by his name, but she reverently calls him Mr. Bachchan, the way she used to refer to him when he came to BSS for parent-teacher meetings.

She used to watch reruns after reruns of his movies at the cheapest of cinemas in Bandra West with my father. My father hated Mr. Bachchan with a searing white-hot hatred. But to be with Mama and please her, he used to watch his movies. Amitabh Bachchan was the man Papa could never be, especially at that most crucial hour, when Mama needed him the most, when it was time for me to have taken center stage in their lives.

I buy a new Amitabh Bachchan coffee table book whenever I go to Granth. It's my Amitabh Bachchan place; he stays a few kilometers away in a bungalow called Jalsa.

It's for my mama. For a man she reveres more than my father; a man who, she feels, is always so right.

My father too was so right a match in the beginning, but then I came along, bloody me, and I ruined my mama's marriage. I took her true love from her.

The least I can do is gift her photographs and books of the one she can still be close to, in a vague sort of way.

The wind carries your old love to me and sets my memory working,
I'm growing old and my time is near, though I think I remember you as you were;
I will never forget you, for you are in the arteries red as my soul's echo,
See a star is fading away and is passing on even more light when it happens.

I see so many celebrities at Granth. I hope one day I'll see my mama's Mr. Bachchan.

the victoria's

I was traveling one day on Lady Jamshedji Marg, Mahim, when the taxi stopped at the signal near Our Lady of Victories Church. I looked out of the window, and I saw that the old Secondhand and Lending Library named Victoria's Circulating Library was now two independent lending libraries. It was obvious they had split.

In spite of studying at BSS for nearly twelve years, I had never been to the Victoria library, as my school library was more than enough in addition to the comics from Step-In. Now I was intrigued. I wondered, *Why not?* and got out to investigate along with Blaise.

Due to unknown circumstances, yes indeed, this circulating library cum secondhand bookshop had split and was being run by two different people. I checked out both collections and liked them.

In fact, I loved their paperbacks from the 1970s and 1980s, which were going cheap, especially the thriller and horror genre books, which I am quite a sucker for.

I immediately took a book from each shop. Then I went on my way. One book was Dan Brown's *The Lost Symbol* and the other was Hakan Nesser's *The Strangler's Honeymoon*.

I didn't read either and the books were left on my bookstand for a year.

No calls and no reminders came forth from either bookshop so I, like a true coward, never went back. Well, never until the May of 2016, one year after the first time I visited their shops.

It was a hot and busy Saturday morning when the call from one of the circulating libraries came through at last on my cell phone. Yes, the use of the word *cell phone* is deliberate for till then I was one of the few twenty-seven-year olds who were still using a cell phone and NOT a smartphone.

It was one of the storeowners asking me casually and politely whether I wanted to renew my account with them. I thought for a moment and then said, yet again, a very hasty "Why not?" and called my cabbie to head to Mahim.

I returned the old books to their rightful owners and offered to pay the fine, but both said they
were just happy I came back. That touched me to
the core—and rarely anything does—but yes, I
was enamored yet again by their paperbacks and
other books in old covers.

I paid a year's fee. I took two books written by
Ruskin Bond from one and two books by Dan
Brown from the other.

I've been going there practically every week
since.

The two bookshops is in a place where, like
Bandra West, there is a huge reading population
filled with various needs that are fulfilled by circulating libraries and secondhand bookstalls. I
never did get down to why the enterprise, which
according to my mama was there even before she
joined BSS forty-five years ago, had split.

Both the stores smell of mosquito repellant
camphor lit sticks and sometimes camphor balls
or mothballs, which I now associate with the
amazing place.

It is amazing. The books are the usual Penguin
and HarperCollins bestsellers from over the
years. I sometimes buy some bestsellers from
there at prices starting at ₹20, which is a steal.
Whenever I want to read some run-of-the-mill

thriller or old classic courtroom drama, or a bit of chick lit, I go to Victoria's. It helps churn my brain and mix it well so that I'm always fresh to start a new short story or essay.

If I am having a spot of bother or a student hassle at the tutorial, I pack up and go there to smell the incense sticks of sandalwood or jasmine and old books. Going through their books is my stress buster, and the fact I go there so often these days means that I am quite stressed out. Back in 2016, when I was penning my LGBTQ collection of short stories called *The Love That Dare Not Speak Its Name,* I visited Victoria's quite often.

For the LGBTQ book, I had to do an extensive amount of armchair research, getting into the minds of my characters who were being abused for no fault of their own. Doing so resulted in giving me a heck of a lot of tension, stress, and anxiety. Most of my research was done during the late hours in the night till 4:00 a.m., and sometimes even 8:00 a.m. I was like a possessed being and closer to becoming a vampire than I'll ever be again.

Victoria's simplicity and affordability helped me to release that pent-up stress.

Soon both owners learned to trust me and give me all the books I wanted. They are gracious, business like but aware of the book trade. I've spent some of my best days reading their awesome used books by Stephen King, Dan Brown, Erle Stanley Gardener, Jeffery Archer, James Patterson, Mary Higgins Clarke, Neil Gaiman, David Baldacci, Lee Child, John Grisham, Ken Follett, Jo Nesbo, Harlan Coben, Danielle Steel, Sidney Sheldon, Dean Koontz, Robin Cook, and Tess Gerritsen.

As I said, I'm a sucker for thrillers.

The stores are in a Hindu-Muslim-Christian area, and whenever all three are put together you can be sure there will be chaos—and normally there is chaos here. Trust Mahim to have a church, Hindu mandir/temple as well as a Muslim masjid all in the same area.

The circulating libraries themselves are near the famous Sitladevi temple. Let me add here that both the stores are run by Muslims. And that near the bookstore is the church. This can happen only in India: cows grazing by the temple's entrance, with mosque, and church nearby.

The women who sit at the temple's entrance with their cows now know me well and look at each other when I carry off a jute bag full of books to the waiting taxi. This place is rife with any number of stories, fodder for my imaginative mind; especially the middle-aged married women of all denominations visiting Victoria's.

Due to the construction of the Mumbai Metro, the place is hell where it comes to traffic during peak hours. Both the owners think I must be barking mad to come all the way from Bandra West to Mahim just to go through some old books. But then they don't know the "violence of my affection" towards books (when I say this, I am quoting Mr. Collins in *Pride and Prejudice*, which according to me is the most overrated book I have ever read!).

Yet, in the middle of the continuous day and night, and all of its clanging and banging, I still find Victoria's to be a real stress buster. I relate it with action of the peaceful kind.

I sell my old books there. I make a good sum out of it. The readers get something good to read, and we are all happy!

I save that money for the month of May, the month where we don't get any tuition money at all. Some parents are generous and pay. Others pretend that we teachers live on air during the month of May. I have been spending my May holidays most of the time cruising around Victoria's. The place grounds me. It makes me feel, yet again, protected, but not completely as it's not like a fortress but a café where you can go inside, browse in peace, and maybe visit the church, temple, or masjid according to your faith on your way homeward.

It has a very R. K. Narayan type of setting, rustic yet intimate.

But things aren't doing well. Amazon is on the rise and secondhand bookshops are not doing as well as they used to.

I'm afraid that ... I don't even want to type the words that I fear the most. I have heard that one of the Victoria's may be closing their bookstore or moving into another line of business

Seriously, why can't clothing shops close down or stores selling makeup that make us look more like monkeys than we already are?

Why can't the many restobars shut down? Why not places where they do up your hair to look like a Christmas tree? Why can't they shut down that never-ending noise on the Mahim main roads because of the Metro—clang-bang-clang-bang-clang-clang-bang-bang-da-da-da-dam! It sounds like an old USSR propaganda video, you know? The ones about working at the factory and all!

For now, there is succor here. I don't know how long secondhand bookstores are going to last. But if this place ... I'll miss it more than I'll miss the death of Lopez the cat who scratched me last month, I can tell you that much. No, really, I'll miss the shops.

Why can't we see that it should not always be the new that has to replace the old?

I do read on the Kindle, I admit. But, it's not the same as a physical, real book. I know it's blasphemous for me to say so, considering I get money for my Kindle books and all. But I still say, it's not the same.

Now, when I go there, I go thinking, will this be the last visit? But I've just got here, just recently discovered it. It's wonderful, why does it have to go?

Why does everyone have to leave me and go?

My father, my father's family, the books from BSS, Mrs. Ratnaswami, Aruna, my nana, my older cats ... and who knows who else's departure are just about to break my heart at the next turning of the page.

But, yes, I have had my heart broken many times. Even though this heart of mine is filled with printer's black ink and the walls of hand-made paper.

And once my heart was broken by a bookstore itself, which shut down forever on February 27, 2018.

It was the Strand Book Stall at Fort in town.

It was the Mecca of book lovers in Mumbai. We let it happen, but I had something to take away from it even then.

the strand and the man called shanbhag

When Blaise used to pick up books for me to read, I read them but never asked where he got them. The day he told me, I was seventeen years old. Yes, I know, that's kind of laid-back for a bookworm or a book phoenix, but do remember that I am a solitary soul, the quiet type, and that even today I know next to nothing about my father's family.

That was the day Blaise told me about a man called Shanbhag.

He told me that once Shanbhag had a dream. His dream was to build the best bookstore in Mumbai.

He started out at the Strand Cinema with a shelf or two. Then someone gave him a place in

Fort, the most distant part of Bombay at that time, in the middle of the twentieth-century India, Mumbai. He collected a band of loyal salesmen and taught them to be as dedicated to the book trade as he was.

He taught them to love books and how the customers always came first.

The rest is history. The Strand, which has no connection to its namesake in New York, became the best bookshop in Mumbai, bringing out new boxes of books practically every alternate day.

Blaise told me how years ago the place was always packed like a cinema theater, that it was difficult to breathe sometimes because of the numerous readers collected there to buy books. They sold books at discounted prices all the time, which was the best part about buying at the Strand: excellent discounts and excellent books.

Blaise was an impressionable twenty-something Catholic lad from Bandra West working as a clerk at Bank of India. Blaise had heard of the Strand, the Mecca of book lovers not only in Mumbai but in all of India. He came to the store and made friends with the salesmen.

He couldn't afford the books even at discounted prices back then, in the 1970s and 1980s. He used to sit in a corner and read, and that man, the legendary Shanbhag, never said a word to him.

Blaise sometimes wondered why Shanbhag never said anything to him, though he was sometimes in the way and he did not buy the books, and he was also the last to leave at closing, like the shadow of twilight.

Blaise would get his answer only in February 2018, when an article was printed in the newspapers about Strand closing down and exhorting us to visit it for old time's sake.

It seemed that when Shanbhag was young, he couldn't afford the books he wanted to read at a bookstore, and so used to read in the bookstall itself ... and was once kicked out.

That day he swore an oath that he would create the best bookstore in Mumbai, where young people could stand and read books, even if they couldn't afford to pay his prices. He would not stop any reader from enjoying his books.

This was Shanbhag. He is no more. But his legacy lives on in the people in Mumbai who love books, and in Blaise and me.

Now, coming back to a time when I was nineteen years old, we set off with the whole family, including Rita, my aunt, to the Strand Bookstore, a two-floor "too crammed for space" bookstore at

Fort, near the place where most of the British heritage structures are located and, therefore, thronged with tourists.

Strand, Mecca, my new haunt.

More books.

By the time I discovered the Strand, Shanbhag had already gone to his eternal reward. Most of the earlier salesmen who knew Blaise had left. Blaise didn't have a clue where they had gone, well, not for a few more years until something else wonderful happened. But right now only some of the old workers were still there, holding the flamed torch bravely, as one would say.

I loved the place, but because it was so far away, about sixteen kilometers from home, and we had no conveyance back then, I could visit the shop only on a monthly basis, and that was toward the wee end of its majestic but bravely fought existence.

I loved the old hardbacks there. I discovered my first taste for Dennis Wheatley books and books on historical topics that I was studying at St. Andrews College. Mama loved the Strand too, but she had an inkling that our joy wouldn't last.

The salesmen present were too silent. As the years floated by, the crowds stopped coming. New books stopped arriving. I still went there but realized that no new books were coming in, and no one was buying the old ones. My heart ached as I left the place, empty-handed.

"Stop going there," Mama cautioned me. "I need you to be happy."

I looked the other way, denying the fact with the following retort: "It's the least I can do for Shanbhag." Yet again, strangely, another man that I never knew, or even meet in person, was vital to my life. I couldn't stop going, and yet Mama was right: I also couldn't bear to see a bookshop dying.

"Uncle, when will the new books come?" I sat in front of the oldest of the salesmen who had remained with the store till its last year. That was in November of 2017.

He looked at me with a weak smile that pleaded for something. There were tears in his old, wrinkled gray eyes.

His eyes told me the truth.

I left that time with a few books about St. Francis of Assisi and St. Theresa of Avila. As I walked out, I said a prayer to both. It was a prayer consisting of only three words: "Not Shanbhag too."

On a hot February day in 2018, I knew that the Catholic saints don't listen to prayers of girl children and bookworms or, for that matter, book phoenixes.

It appeared in the newspaper. The Strand's last day would be the twenty-seventh of February. We still had a few days left. Shanbhag's daughter requested its old patrons to adopt at least one book from the shelves to keep it safe and give it a home, just like Shanbhag once let books enter our lives and the Strand which was his 'home' he made ours.

I cried. Blaise cried. He more than me, I swear!

We bought a book each. I bought John Galsworthy's omnibus. I can't remember what Blaise bought. I just remember him looking around the place, which had come to life again thanks to the news article.

The last clarion call was heard. Patrons came in great numbers.

Shanbhag lived again. The Strand lived for one week, buzzing with customers and action like its good old self.

"Is this how it used to look?" I asked Blaise as we slowly made our way to the fiction shelves. He nodded emphatically with tears.

They came in large groups, they came in cabs and cars, young and old to bid Shanbhag's Strand a final goodbye.

"A memento, please, Uncle! I begged one of the salesmen," but he was too overcome with grief. I had hoped for a poster or a pamphlet.

"Anything, please, Uncle, I won't be coming here again! Memento please, Uncle!"

The salesman, weary with age and sorrow, did not respond. So Blaise and I did it the smartphone generation's way. We took selfies. We took selfies of ourselves, our purchases, and the Strand with its shutters up.

The media arrived to document the event, as there had never been such an overwhelming crowd of people before. We left in the taxi without any more fuss.

We thought that was the end of it.

The twenty-seventh of February came, and the shutters of the Strand shut forever.

Again, we thought that was the end of it.

But I guess Shanbhag from his afterlife abode was looking out for me. Maybe he heard through all the fog and denseness of illusions, my cry, a mad book lady's cry for "memento."

I guess he wanted to adopt me. Because something like magic happened somewhere during the month of March, after my twenty-ninth birthday.

*

What was the Strand to me?

What was Shanbhag to me?

And that bookstore of his that provided me with my Goosebumps, classics, encyclopedias, and history books when my school library did not provide me with what I needed?

What was the Mecca Shanbhag created but a heritage of the best of books for my godfather and younger maternal uncle, Blaise, which he passed down to me?

St. Francis of Assisi and St. Teresa of Avila may have forgotten my devotion to them and their writings.

Or had they?

I tell you, sometimes when miracles happen like the one that happened to me that March, you tend to want to believe in that God of Moses all over again.

We got the news that the Strand Book Stall's Burma teakwood bookstands were FOR SALE!

I'll dwell on how we found that out in another essay. But the moment Blaise and I heard the news, which we wouldn't have heard at all if it were not for pure luck and chance, we drove to Strand, and as a memento, my last final wish, at last, we bought four bookstands from the Strand.

Yes, four Burma teakwood stands, solid as a rock, bereft of books (only until my own collection filled them up once the delivery men brought them home).

We installed three of them at my modest 1 BHK flat. The smallest and last we installed in my office-cum-writing hut.

Today, I live, breathe, and work in the very presence of Shanbhag, my name for all my book-shelves stuffed full with books on nature, wildlife, politics, sociology, medicine, philosophy, literary fiction, graphic novels, and much more.

My birthday month was made more blessed with this out-of-the-way dream come true.

Strange how it seemed that the place loved me so much that it wanted to come home with me.

Strange that today the very shelves I normally used to peruse during my time at the Strand are now right in my bedroom.

Strange that a piece of Mecca came to my humble home and made me, little existentialist me, believe in the power of love. Love of the word. To my right, as I write, is my chota (small) Shanbhag. Thank you for choosing to adopt me, Shanbhag, by allowing me to adopt you. May we always be together, for the rest of our lives.

Thank you to the Fates, destiny, and the little things that make greater miracles. Thank you for giving me a new uncle, Uncle Shanbhag.

A place gave me a part of itself. By giving of itself, it gave me forever what I will always feel for the books at Strand—the love of a fatherless daughter.

*

You know. When I sleep alone in my bedroom due to exhaustion or unbearable pain due to spondylosis, in my half awake-half dream state, all the time I feel the patting of a man's soothing wrinkled but tender hands on my head and my hunchback. I hear a man's voice speaking a strange dialect, something like old Konkani, the one spoken by Hindus.

I somehow know that the man is telling me to take it easy, that he is there for me, and that I should rest for a while.

I understand and yet I do not understand. It's just something that I sense.

When I asked Blaise what all this was, he told me Shanbhag used to talk in Konkani to his staff.

kitab khana

The Strand Book Stall used to be the Mecca of all Mumbai book lovers.

It was the conception of a man called Shanbhag. He had a brood of salesmen faithful to him in his lifetime.

But then most of the younger salesmen were displaced when Strand Book Stall was downsized after Mr. Shanbhag's death. These salesmen came together, like the Phoenix, in new garb and with new life at Kitab Khana Bookstore, Somaiya Bhavan, Mumbai.

It is near the heritage structure of Flora Fountain in town. The Hindi words, *Kitab Khana*, mean "The Place of Books," and we came to know of it through word of mouth.

For the first visit, we took our own private cabbie, so the journey was easy. Somaiya Bhavan was famous, and Kitab Khana was the venture of a woman who came from a business family from Somaiya.

It is a beautiful place, assembled aesthetically and with a better system of workers and managers than most bookstores.

The place retained some of the old nineteenth-century structures like its ancient staircase, Victorian statues of beautiful asexual beings, floor-to-ceiling bookshelves, Muslim columns with gothic look, Parsee marble round tables, and shining marble floors.

Kitab Khana, as you walk into it, has its own smell, which is delicious to the nostrils of a book lover.

The place is a feast for the eyes, and it has a café. What more could one need?

It was here at Kitab Khana, looking at the latest books on display, that I decided I one day was going to be a writer. That was back in 2010.

Kitab Khana was the place I went to most often, the place my best books were bought, where I met and, yes, befriended not only books but human beings as well. I still dance like a plus-size ballerina when I enter the place. I feel like a princess of old when I climb the floor-to-ceiling steps necessary to get to the classic section. I look at the wooden high ceiling and little wind chimes seem to tingle their sweet song in my ears.

You can't help but be happy in such a lively place packed with the world's choicest books ever!

Kitab Khana has made me the writer and publisher I am today. I associate the place with my adulthood, the prime of my life, almost every other free weekend of my entire third decade has been spent at Kitab Khana buying and hugging these beautiful and erudite books. I am twenty-nine years old. Kitab Khana is nine years young. Next year it hits a decade, and I then am officially, without any doubt, too old to be called Mama's little girl.

The world seems right with you by my side,
A bookshop like home wherever I go;
You've made my world complete to dream a song in
ink,
Beautiful book of words so bright that the light may
never fade.

I had my very first book, *S.O.S Animals and Other Stories*, on display right here. It was my first book launch, my first foray into the world of letters, my first book reading, my first bookshop where my book *Classics* became a bestseller in 2017; where business deals are still made and old relations become richer like old red wine.

Kitab Khana is my real second home; it has taken the place of Mrs. Ratnaswami's library now devoid of its heritage of books. Oh, Kitab Khana, if there is a heaven I hope it looks like you.

So many memories, all so sweet like brown sugar, or Gur, is what Kitab Khana is to me. I may be going on thirty, but I can still remember that girl of twenty-one who entered its vast expanse and was consumed by it.

Kitab Khana, my ecstasy and my pride and my joy—may we always be together even when we are apart.

I am mad with the love of books and your humble shelves,
How has this heart of mine ever lived without you, my ink;
I have lost my senses to words that bring me to the brink then back,
You have become my life, love and have made the two add up to a lifetime.

I've entered a girl and maybe, if all goes well, will come out from there when I am an old woman. For now, an old woman of thirty is the target, and I have so many more books still to read.

Tourists, the middle class, the poor, school students, professors, famous writers, struggling writers, award-winning writers all come and go like the pulsating of blood through an artery. The place is always active, especially during the Kala Godha Festival of the Arts, where they showcase artistic talent to the public.

When I sit in an easy chair by the magazine section, I wonder what would have become of me if it were not for the guidance, patience and support of the people, the books, and the place Kitab Khana itself?

Nothing. I would have been an ordinary teacher in some school, correcting papers and collecting dust like some of the silver fish in my office-cum-writing hut. And then what choice would I have had but to brush away my life into a bin, where sometimes I throw my used-up ball-point pens and rough paper full of useless doodling.

"Where you are dotted, there you are knotted" is an old saying of my family. Never was it so applicable to life than in the case of Kitab Khana.

For, you see, I really wouldn't have done anything with writing and publishing if it weren't for circumstances.

Kitab Khana, through its dedication to books, made me read many books that educated me, and they helped to make me a thinking individual. I bought my very first book on Existentialism here and a short biography on Descartes, two texts which have helped to define me as a person, apart from the bookish side of me, a person who feels that everything is riddled with opposites and questions like: What is truth and what isn't? These were my thoughts then, and they are my thoughts now.

The history section of the bookshop quenched my thirst for good books on the topics I was studying and wanted to learn more about. The Indian National Movement, the foreign policy of Pakistan, the genesis of radical Islam, the Arab Spring, the idea of being a Hindu, studies on the history of Jerusalem, mammoth works on Dalit studies, important Indian women writers of the past, the Bible as fact or fiction, Descartes's values, the Reformation movement in the church, Kant's philosophy, and so much else that made me stop and think, and enriched my life in more ways than one.

But then I left my teaching job at the Lilavati Podar. I was not satisfied because I really wanted to do more. I wanted to write and develop my tutorial. But more than all that, I was hurting.

I was hurting because I, after completion of my teacher's training, was not taken on as a teacher at BSS. I was heartbroken, shattered, and quite unsettled. I had staked all my hopes on getting in, and everyone thought I would. I, it seems, am a pretty good English teacher, but then it happened and I couldn't understand why.

Soon after, I got into Lilavati Podar, another ICSE school, which all said and done I liked, but I was hurting. And I was twenty-one years old, with ambitions to be a writer as well as a teacher.

I had to quit my Podar job simply because I was tired of running away from myself. I needed to focus and get things straight. What did I want to be: a teacher or a writer, or maybe, you know, both?

In the summer of 2012, after I quit my job at Podar, I started writing a novel about a single mother of two girls that I didn't finish. It wasn't all that good.

I then tried to write a few more parable stories in longhand, but they didn't hit a cord within me either.

But then my book *S.O.S Animals and Other Stories* was published by CreateSpace Amazon in the month of August. I had written this book in my last year at college, in 2009, during free lectures. It was my very first "for real" book. Ever since I published it, there has been no looking back.

I had put my hand to the plow, I had made the right choice. Now to see it through, I had to stick by it, let old demons die over time, and work very, very, very hard.

Today, I'm twenty-nine and funding my own publishing company. I'm a multiple award-winning writer. And Kitab Khana has been with me through it all, in the form of love, in the form of total support.

They have given me confidence to stand up in front of an audience of readers and not stammer or say something stupid. I've been interviewed often. I've appeared in a documentary called *Black Sheep* by Reshel Shah Kapoor, which was about the Kinnar transsexual community of India, especially Mumbai, which lead me to pen my book, *The Love That Dare Not Speak Its Name: Short Stories*, which has received positive trade reviews as well as publishing awards.

I have won many accolades and awards for my books.

But this was because of the choices I made with the help of the people who loved me the most—my family and the bookshops I have patronized, especially Kitab Khana, whose salesmen and managers were the very people who were with Shanbhag and who were Blaise's friends.

It was there, in their store in March that we were told about the Strand bookshelves that were being sold.

Blaise and I were at Kitab Khana on business to talk about *Nirmala: The Mud Blossom,* which we were planning to release in Mumbai, when this lawyer came up to us and made one single statement: "You know that the Strand is selling its bookshelves?"

That was all he said. Then he went deeper into the Kitab Khana bookstore and was lost in the crowd.

I didn't see him at all after that. It was like he just vanished into book dust.

"Is it true, really?" I asked, completely taken aback with too much joy. And the managers of Kitab Khana said, "Yes," and that the bookshelves were real Burma teakwood.

That very minute, Blaise and I rushed out of the place to drive to the Strand. I looked around for the lawyer, my ambiguous angel in disguise to thank him, but I didn't see him anywhere.

No matter, we sped away, and with the blessings of Shanbhag's daughter, Vidya, we bought four of the bookshelves, especially the one which is the oldest in the store, which used to showcase the latest books that had come to the store and were in the market.

And Shanbhag came home. After all these long years of complacency, I finally met the prophet of Mecca. All this thanks to a lawyer, smartly dressed and of medium-sized frame with a slender waist, who I look out for every time I am at Kitab Khana, but I have yet to trace him.

You can meet angels in Kitab Khana, too.

Has my hurting ceased? No, but it has lessened.

Have I found the real direction my life was supposed to take? I don't think so, but I'm juggling with so many things right now that a casual onlooker, upon seeing my life, would say, "This woman has got *way* too much on her plate right now. More than she wished for."

Kitab Khana introduced me to publishers. And now they introduce other publishers to me as a young budding director of Fiza Pathan Publishing. I'll just take it as it comes, one book at a time, because that's what Kitab Khana's success has taught me—one book at a time, one day at a time.

I started here as a young adult and since that time, I've become a woman. And I don't know what more is in store for me.

So many books have turned me into the woman I am. I can't name them all, because doing so would require a catalog. But I think the saying is true where Kitab Khana is concerned: "It is only when you buy a book that you become richer with the purchase."

And I think that is so true where this bookstore is concerned. It makes you take books and their writers seriously. The Kitab Khana team has made me realize that it's okay to be a writer, to be confident and say it loud and proud: I am a writer. I have the magical power of making you disappear into my stories.

What's your magic power?

wayword and wise

discovered this bookstore, specially curated for the elite, via word of mouth. We knew, after the shutting down of the Strand and so many other stores, like the famous good old Rhythm House near Kala Godha and five minutes walking distance from Strand, that something new was coming up. Something bookish.

And we were right. Wayword and Wise came up on the road near the bustling Chhatrapati Shivaji Terminus. And it's chic, dignified, and charming.

Like Kitab Khana, it has its own alluring smell, the smell of books fresh from the press. If only we could get these magnificent smells bottled as perfumes, (sigh)! But we can't get everything, can we? We do get good erudite books, and that's close enough.

The manager is an old acquaintance of Blaise's and worked in other reputed bookstores like the Strand, Crossword, and Lotus Book House, the last of which closed down just before I finished school and I regret not getting a chance to patronize it. It was located on S.V. Road near the Mahim causeway junction. I am so very unfortunate!

My taste in books has been upgraded thanks to Wayword and Wise. I found the place when I was an established publisher. It was a pleasure to hear the manager ask for my card and me taking it out, gracefully, like some of these rich, well-dressed women do and daintily dropping the card into the glass bowl kept aside for that purpose alone.

The bookstore is frequented by poetry lovers and eccentric artists, big and small, like me (the small) who want to buy rarities. For that is what the franchise specializes in; rare books of good quality which you can't get anywhere else, in addition to the regular, new good stuff.

When I'm there, I feel elegant, in vogue and full of fine tastes.

My love for reading poetry began there, and I also started developing my craft by reading the experiences of other famous writers and their essays.

I read Helene Hanff's *41 Charing Cross Road* in 2016 and have not been the same again.

I have had some good and erudite conversations with the manager. He has an insatiable hunger for books, just like me. He got me to appreciate so many writers, especially their essays. He is very helpful but also leaves me to myself, knowing that I'm not the kind who likes to talk a lot.

He talks more to Blaise, about business, about the good old or bad old days, about the books then and now, and so much else as I browse the shelves feeling at peace with the world and myself as Beethoven's symphonies play softly on the sound system in the background.

I come here often to feel that which I can never be. Which my poor father too can never be.

I mentioned earlier that sometimes he crawls out from under the rock that I've placed over him and makes his paternity known. These days, it is to do with the money he wants to give me. The money that for all these years he has been keeping aside for me, apparently, so that he with a clear conscience can go for his Haj.

"Fiza beta, take my money, please.

"Fiza beta, all this money is for you. I'm an old man. Do me a favor and take it now.

"Fiza beta, your papa needs to go in peace.

"Fiza beta, take what is yours and let me go.

"Fiza ... beta. ..."

He never even calls me *beti*, which means daughter in Hindi. He calls me *beta*, which means *son*. I hate this endearment, even though I have forgiven him for what he has done to Mama.

So he wants to do something which he should have done a heck of a long time ago: spend money on my upkeep, his only child. But I've never received a penny from him, and I do not want any of it now.

But the man is insistent, and absolutely intolerable!

"Fiza beta, please take the money and let me go for my Haj.

"Fiza beta, Papa is asking you this. I'm your Papa, yes Fiza beta?

"Fiza beta, I'll die if you don't take the money. Papa is asking, beta.

"Fiza – Fiza – Fiza!"

When I am irritated with his stupid messages and calls, I come to Wayword and Wise, to show my father that, here, look, *the stone that you rejected has become the corner stone dear papa of mine! And I don't want your bloody money. No amount of money can undo the tears my mama has shed for you, tears I have shed for you!*

I've changed my number. But he calls on the landline.

I have read many rare books about Islam and Mecca here at Wayword and Wise. What my father has done to Mama and me, Islam prohibits vehemently. Then what sort of holy pilgrimage and blood money does this wretched old man want to push down my throat? What kind of pilgrimage condones the sins of the father upon the wife he said he loved and the daughter he and his family rejected because of gender? I do not know this God, the God who hates infant girls.

Who is this God who hates women?

I see him, this God who hates women, in the books about women's issues, in the tenets of all religions I've ever studied, and even in the very cells I am made of and of which I am ashamed.

When I am ashamed of myself and what my father has done to Mama and me, I come here. It makes me realize that girls, too, can be sons, and can easily mingle with the rich and famous but silently; an anonymous person who only loves books and who is reclusive, unless it's time to buy a new book.

I've grown reclusive these past two years. I spend most of my time either teaching or writing here, in my office-cum-writing hut. I've lived a good life as a youth, and I've earned my keep for the most part. I've searched in books for a reason but have found answers that clarifies other questions with more doubts for yet another foray into Wayword and Wise.

My adulting, as they call it, began here. I am no longer the girl I was, neither am I the young teacher nor the budding writer I once was.

I have aged like the old heritage buildings surrounding Wayword and Wise. But my days are full of activity, again like the trainloads of office goers emerging from CST station and moving all over the place, along with a few tourists, who drop into the bookstore for the love of the ambience and to pour over the hardback treasures they have heard so much about in blog posts on the internet.

I look ahead and I cannot see what the future holds. I have so much more to do and so little time on earth to do so. I've so many stories to tell, and so much more to do for my family members, who have accepted my love for books, libraries, and bookshops the same way I accept the pretty moths that die on my books at my office-cum-writing hut.

They sing their song for one summer and then die; so, too, one day will I.

These things I contemplate while reading a book of essays by John Updike or Albert Camus bought full price from Wayword and Wise, which smells of new books and new discoveries every day and every time I visit the store.

my office-cum-writing hut

It was when I was researching and writing the stories that would go on to become *The Love That Dare Not Speak Its Name* that I struck a gold mine.

I was still on the lookout for a proper place to write my books. Home was too packed with students practically everywhere. And even though we had rented the neighboring flat from a good neighbor, that place was full of students morning, afternoon, and till late evening. I desperately needed a place to write.

That's when we heard from our trusty electrician that the Muslim tailor near our house was leaving her shop to go elsewhere. The owner of the vacated property wanted a new tenant, and my electrician wanted to know if we were interested. If we were, then he would give us first preference. It seems everyone in Mumbai is on long waiting lists for even the smallest of huts in Bandra West, the Queen of the Suburbs.

Mama was not sure, because there was a coconut tree growing right at the center of the tenement. But I was sure and made the first bid. I rented the place, which became my office and now a writing hut, something cleaner than Roald Dahl's writing hut near his home in England.

Yes, in good, old Ruskin Bond fashion there really is a coconut tree growing almost like a beam or a sturdy pillar through the place. The cutting of trees until under duress is strictly prohibited in Mumbai. Therefore, even though the shanty was being built, the landowner, a rich Maharashtrian of the soil was refused permission to cut the tree.

"Build whatever you want and however you want, but don't cut the tree" was the general idea. Indeed, before our very eyes because our ground floor flat overlooks the writing hut which the landowner constructed in such a way that the roof is strong, the tree given sufficient support so that if there is a storm it will never fall, and no holes or crevices at all. First it was let to a Muslim young tailor whom I spoke about earlier. Then me, a single late 20s writer, poet and publisher.

I have made the office homey with my tastes, something which was not possible at home in our small and pokey 1 BHK. I have divided the hut into two rooms, one much bigger than the other, with a common ceiling. The bigger room is my writing space. The smaller one is to store the books to be sold to the bookstores.

In the smaller room, I've kept a water cooler, a place to make tea without milk, of course, and a lot of chairs, recliners, and an office study table for anyone else working with me.

Normally Blaise, I, and another gentleman called Michaelangelo Zane work in that space and discuss business matters.

The bigger space is my kingdom, and that's where I think, write, type, read, and these days spend most of, if not all, my time.

This place is surrounded by cast-metal book-shelves without glass cover sliding doors for easy access.

"Pizza, I tell you these days people have no value for wooden solid bookshelves," I can al-most hear Mrs. Ratnaswami grumbling at the back of my mind. She loved wooden bookcases, the bookcases made of Burma teakwood, the ones not prone to be eaten by white ants, similar to the book stands I purchased from Shanbhag's Strand

Book Stall. But even Mrs. Ratnaswami had to admit the very first few metal bookshelves to the school library after it increased in size in the year 2000. When she saw the photograph of my bookshelves on Facebook she said, "Your office is like a library itself."

Yes, that's an atmosphere in which I work best.

On the bookshelves, I've placed some curios and certain bric-à-brac to help me if I'm stuck without an idea for what to write. I've been fond of curios for as long as I can remember but couldn't afford them until recently. Now I can manage some. There is a bust of Shakespeare; a plaster of Paris statue of an angel with a book; rubber plastic images of Asterix the Gaul, his best friend Obelix, their druid Getafix, and their crooning bard, Cacofonix; similar rubber plastic images of Tintin the Belgian reporter, his best friend Captain Haddock, their mutual friend Professor Calculus, Snowy the canine sleuth with a bone in his mouth, Nestor the butler with a tray full of spirits nearly toppling over, Bianca Castafiore (with her parrot, which was a get well present to Haddock), Thomson and Thompson standing back-to-back ready for action, and so much more.

I can't get enough of these comic characters.

Then there is an old 1946 Olympia typewriter that still has got ink in it and is functional, a ship in a glass bottle, a globe with a watch which is not working, a bowl of red paper roses where the shell of my late pet snail rests in peace, a vase with fake lilies, a statue of Swami Vivekananda, a colored bust of Shivaji Maharaj, a statue of a bull-dog, a golden retriever, a statue of a potter—making pots—an Indian version of the umbrella man, an angel made of marble with a fake crystal in the palm of its left hand, a reed diffuser with Bergamot lime and geranium oil diffused through it, and so much else.

The books are overflowing the shelves. There is a fountain that runs water like a brook for calming my senses with a statue of St. Francis of Assisi at its center.

There are six shelves reserved for my award medals and certificates, but unfortunately, not all can be displayed. Upon them are the framed photographs of my five favorite writers of all time, which I hold dearer to me than the awards they tower over. I look to them when I am stuck on a difficult scene or a troublesome character. They are R. K. Narayan, Ruskin Bond, B. R. Ambedkar, Munshi Premchand, and William Shakespeare. Of all of them, only Ruskin Bond still lives, whom I hope to meet soon to thank him for his books, his life, and for being an inspiration to a lonely soul in Bandra, especially on loud cracker-bursting Diwali nights.

Around the coconut tree, I used to keep plants, a sort of temple garden with the likes of the black Buddha in lotus position, Mirabai with her veena, and a paper peacock. Money plants, geraniums, bamboos, china grass, white balsam, and so much else used to grow there; but then I couldn't maintain them because my maid met with a serious accident and is now unable to use her leg properly. She was the one who used to clean up and air the plants on weekends while I tended to their needs during the week. So, I brought them all out into my garden. I miss their company.

At the corner near the coconut tree is a small, round table with a chair. It's there where I sit and write and type, where I am typing these words right now.

*

What has my office-cum-writing hut done for me? How has it shaped my personality and my identity? What do I feel when I am here?

To tell you the truth, I've grown roots here, which is in itself a dangerous thing to do for our business is expanding and we need a bigger place.

But I've just got here. This place is where I've slogged, cried, laughed, spoken to myself, contemplated, and smelled the perfume of jasmine from my scented candle.

This place has given me the respect and identity in Bandra West of a fine writer and an even finer teacher of English. When we moved into this place, we made people in the neighborhood realize that even simple teachers like Mama and I can make big dreams a reality.

Even a girl can be a son to her family.

This place has established that fact. The quality writing that Blaise and I produce with our other helpers is a testimony to that, and I'm proud of my achievements.

But I don't want to brag about it; I'm not the type. That's why, though I have represented India, and sometimes Asia, in so many prestigious writing and book competitions, no one knows anything about me.

All people know is that in Bandra West there lives a strange woman or girl who is an excellent English teacher. She is also a writer and doesn't talk much. *But go there. I'm sure she'll help you out.*

Sometimes people in Bandra have such a murky picture of Mama and me that they think we are the same person—my mama being that person. Sometimes the parents of my students are shocked that I even exist.

"But I've never seen you before. Where have you come from?" That's the kind of look they give me when they see me for the first time. I want to say, "Relax guys, I've always been here. Maybe I was caught up in my reading and that's why we've never met—but I'll teach and you can pay me to read more books, and we'll understand each other."

This office is the fruit of my hard-earned money and work ever since I started teaching, nine years ago. It's the symphony of my love for the written word, a temple to my only God, the "Word." The dust of this place hugs my bare feet more dearly than another one's feet, for this is MY dust, MY sweat, and MY blood.

Only a few have I allowed through this door, through this portal, which I have myself crafted into a place suitable to hone my simple art.

I'm no MFA honors student. I'm only qualified to be a history teacher.

Yet, I'm considered a master of Shakespeare, poetry, and prose, which is what I teach to earn my keep. Here I am after all these years of wandering in books, and yet, haven't I always been right here?

This writing hut has made me a self-actualized person, ten percent of such a person. The other ninety percent needs a lot of work. For I am no man in all men. For I am no woman in all women. Vice versa holds true. I'm somebody, yet, I'm nobody.

I'm happy enough with the title of the reclusive writer and reader of the neighborhood. I'm sure I have plenty of other nicknames, but as long as I can roam around here, in my quiet little space, I am content.

Although I forgave my father way back in 2007, it's now in 2018 that I've finally begun to realize what forgiveness really means. It means, just like good old Jesus Christ, or as I call him, JC, said—forgive your neighbor and then come to serve the Lord.

Though I have dedicated this hut spiritually to St. Francis of Assisi, I'm not the God person I used to be. I'm just human now trying not to act like a book when dealing with the people who really matter to me. I don't really pray to God, or beg or question him. I'm just going to read and read and teach and teach and write and write—till eternity, as a prayer to anyone who needs my toil as a prayer. For reading, writing, and teaching is praying to me. And I pray a lot here, in my office-cum-writing hut.

I was always a recluse and a bookworm. I've always been a writer since the day my father deserted me when I was born. It's just that this place has made it official, and all is good for now.

I like when the few close to me visit me here. I like the place especially early in the mornings, when the cuckoo calls out its refrain and the green parrots cackle as they help themselves to berries from the fruit trees.

I like the place when it rains. Pitter—patter—pitter—patter goes the rain, and the old coconut tree doesn't shake. I love the smell of wet earth, as long as it is all happening outside. I despise water falling from the sky on a general basis, and I certainly don't like getting wet. Especially not getting my books wet!

This place is my fortress, my castle, where I spend my day without minding anyone's business. I hope to spend good times here more than anywhere else in the world. For this is bliss, the only heaven I know.

ruskin bond's hills

would like to end this series of essays with something different.

This pertains to a place or places, places I have never been but have visited through the narratives of India's favorite writer, the writer from the hills, Ruskin Bond of Mussoorie, Landour.

Since I was a little wee thing, I've loved Ruskin Bond's stories about the hills of India; the Himalayas naturally is what I am referring to here. I've always been stuck here in the city. In the city that never sleeps, where I can't hear the birds that I wish to hear, except the incessant crow that caws at me every time I open the office door.

Then there is, day and night, the incessant sound of scooters, cars, rickshaws, taxies honking away even in the dead of night. To be frank, even when I traveled to Meshu's place on the 24th of September for her seventieth birthday, I was stuck in traffic at 11:00 p.m. in the bloody night! A full traffic jam with honking and swearing and a lot of petrol fumes despite traveling in an air-conditioned cab.

Pathetic, I know. But, ah! the hills!

"You must be mad!" says Mama, every time I mention buying a holiday home in the hill stations up north, the closer to the hills the better. "Why, you will catch your death of cold; yes, you will. No, no, just buy another place in Bandra and be happy with it."

"I was hoping to buy one place in Thane and the other for my holiday home in Landour, Mussoorie," I say gruffly while browsing through a stack of books I want to read.

My mama and Meshu holler, "You don't want to live in Mumbai? You actually want to live in Thane and Mussoorie! THERE ARE FORESTS THERE. YOU WILL BE EATEN BY A LEOPARD! People are dying for Mumbai, and this our girl wants to go to the jungle to become Mowgli!"

But all said and done, it's a damn fact I want to go north. I'd rather put up with a spotted leopard or a black panther right out of a Ruskin Bond book than stay for the rest of my life near that blessed Arabian Sea. No! Never! I want land and I want it all around me, and quite high!

In any case Mumbai is going under water according to all reports. So are the coastal areas, so what's wrong in investing cheap and higher up? The Himalayas are quite higher up, I assure you.

I love nature. I love the simple way of life. And if that's what the hill stations of India are all about, then there I will go. For me, the hills mean only one single thing, and that is my true home.

I've never been completely at home in Mumbai. It's never called out to me as much as the hills have. And I hope that my last days of retirement are spent there in the Himalayas, in a quiet locality, and in a flat or cottage of my own, where I can read and can actually walk down the street peacefully without always 24/7 being on my guard about who is about to run me over from all directions. I mean really now, Mumbai is getting pathetic where the traffic rules and the population is concerned.

Mama says, "Why not buy another house in Bandra West as your holiday home away from home? Everyone is doing that."

Do you see any sense in that at all? Well, I certainly don't. I've been a land lover for as long as I know. All that Conrad and R. L. Stevenson and

Moby Dick stuff is quite all right in books BUT NOT IN REAL LIFE! I am a hill woman and to the hills I shall go.

Who is the culprit? We can hardly call Ruskin Bond a culprit. Let's just say mentor and fellow lover of the hills. That's something that every reader in India associates with the hills, Ruskin Bond, mentor to many a writer and friend to all children who grew up reading his stories of leopards, blue umbrellas, walnut trees, pine cones, hill school boarding houses, hill station life, man-eating tigers, red geraniums, and pet monkeys.

The mountains are in Ruskin Bond's blood, as he has lived there all his life. This is so even though he is an Anglo-Indian. The mountains are in my blood, because even though I've only read about it, the place seems mightily familiar to me. When I think of it, it all seems just right. And that I am going home one day. Someday soon.

Away from all the prying eyes of all the wonderful aunties and uncles of Bandra, back to the hills where I belong.

I know that I know no one in the north. My maternal family and the rest of my so-called cousins are here in Mangalore, down south in Karnataka. But even though I am a R. K. Narayan fan, I don't much care for South Indian life. I really feel it in Ruskin Bond's tales of the hills, like the umbilical cord of a mother to her fetus.

Far from my past and forward into a new future. Maybe I'll be able to talk freely and make friends without benefits, which is the norm of city life, which I loathe, even though I am supposedly a businesswoman.

And a businessman's only child.

"You are just like your paternal grandfather, Ibrahim, right? That was his name?" said Blaise casually one day.

I have no clue, I didn't know the man. And I don't care about blood ties. Only printers' ink and paper. And if I can find a place near the snow-capped mountains with a good recliner in which to read my books, then ever the better. Then I feel that I have been adequately compensated for a lifetime without a father, a father who was not worth the bother.

I don't hate him. I don't want anything from him. To me, he died the day I realized I was being sired by a single mother because I was a girl.

And that was what we had started with, didn't we?

So away I will go to the tall, lofty hills someday. I'll take no memories except for the books that have been my soul mates over the years.

To do this, I'll have to uproot some of my ties with the people in my life.

I have already started to do so. Cut people out of my life. Become more reclusive and away from it all. Because I don't want to leave any tears that will trace the way back to where I want to go.

I have lofty and eccentric ambitions about a place I don't know. And yet, I believe it is my ultimate home.

Hush my tender love this night,
Tomorrow will dawn a new light;
Bear some more this pattering life,
And then to the hills where your heart delights.

Hey, I can dream, can't I?

***

Fiza Pathan has a bachelor's degree in arts from the University of Mumbai, where she majored in history and sociology with a first class. She also has a bachelor's degree in education, again with a first class, her special subjects being English and history.

Fiza has written twelve award-winning books and a short story, which reflect her interest in furthering the cause of education and in championing social issues. In over seventy literary competitions, she has placed either as winner or finalist.

This year she has placed in fifteen literary awards, chief among them: 2018 Digital Book World Winner Best Book (Short Stories); 2018 Digital Book World Finalist Best Book (Social Issues); Killer Nashville 2018 Silver Falchion Award Finalist Best Short Story; 2018 IAN Book Of The Year Awards Winner - Outstanding Fiction LGBTQ; 2018 Montaigne Medal Finalist (Part of Eric Hoffer Award); 2018 Shelf Unbound Competition for Best Independently Published Book - Notable Indie; and 2018 Dan Poynter's Global E-book Awards Winner (Silver Medal).

She lives with her maternal family, and writes novels and short stories in most genres. You may follow her on Twitter @FizaPathan Amazon link: http://www.amazon.com/Fiza-Pathan/e/B0091BCNTU

Website: http://fizapathanpublishing.org/

Mama